Many Lives

Many Lives

Stephanie Beacham

with Owen Smith

HAY HOUSE

Australia • Canada • Hong Kong • India
South Africa • United Kingdom • United States

First published RONDO ured in 21/02/2012 gdom by:
Ha House UK Ltd, 292B Kensal Rd, London W10 5BE.
Tel.: (44) 20 8962 1230; Fax: (44) 20 8962 1239.
www.hayhouse.co.uk

Published and distributed in the United States of America by:
Hay House, Inc., PO Box 5100, Carlsbad, CA 92018-5100.
Tel.: (1) 760 431 7695 or (800) 654 5126; Fax: (1) 760 431 6948 or (800) 650 5115.
www.hayhouse.com

Published and distributed in Australia by:
Hay House Australia Ltd, 18/36 Ralph St, Alexandria NSW 2015.
Tel.: (61) 2 9669 4299; Fax: (61) 2 9669 4144.
www.hayhouse.com.au

Published and distributed in the Republic of South Africa by:
Hay House SA (Pty), Ltd, PO Box 990, Witkoppen 2068.
Tel./Fax: (27) 11 467 8904. www.hayhouse.co.za

Published and distributed in India by:
Hay House Publishers India, Muskaan Complex, Plot No.3, B-2,
Vasant Kunj, New Delhi – 110 070. Tel.: (91) 11 4176 1620; Fax: (91) 11 4176 1630.
www.hayhouse.co.in

Distributed in Canada by:
Raincoast, 9050 Shaughnessy St, Vancouver, BC V6P 6E5.
Tel.: (1) 604 323 7100; Fax: (1) 604 323 2600

© Stephanie Beacham, 2011

The moral rights of the author have been asserted.

A catalogue record for this book is available from the British Library.

Hardback ISBN: 978-1-84850-595-7
Paperback ISBN: 978-1-84850-829-3

Printed and bound by CPI Group (UK) Ltd, Croydon, CR0 4YY

MIX
Paper from
responsible sources
FSC® C020471

A Foreword from Jude

I think that my 'Glamma' is a hard-working, thoughtful and loving grandma. The most loved being to a grandson, as she well knows. But because of her heart, she is making it through life well-mannered, wise, and smart to become not just an outstanding actress, but also an amazing grandma. I usually spend time with her in Malibu, but because of this book there have been quite a few twists. She wakes up at 4 a.m. to write it. She looks like a monster in the morning: swamp green skin, tired eyes and witch-like hair. It is giving me nightmares, but usually she is one of the most glamorous people I've ever seen. I love her with all my heart, and when you read this book you will, too. This is Stephanie Beacham's many lives.

Jude Penny (age 11)

Jude, photographed by Judy Geeson

Contents

Foreword

This is an excellent autobiography, enjoyable to read, beautifully observed and intelligently written with three streams. There is the great actress of stage and screen, the devoted mother and the perfect textbook on how to apply spiritual love in everyday material life.

Like millions of others I have for many years admired Stephanie's performances in all forms of the art, though, admittedly, have often been distracted by her beauty.

When I was told that she would be coming into *Coronation Street* to have a relationship with my alter ego I was absolutely thrilled, over the moon, but also a little nervous. She had done it all – acted with the greats and was a totally dedicated, through-and-through professional. She also had a reputation as a no-nonsense actress, which is something I respect.

We started filming by the canal in the freezing cold. My dog was supposed to fall in the water and Stephanie would rescue her from her barge. The film crew had to break the ice, and then realized that it would be too cold for the dog. So they tried throwing in a stuffed one, but it looked ridiculous and everyone burst out laughing. We got on well. I immediately felt safe with Stephanie – there was something reassuring and comforting about her.

A replica of the barge was built for the interior scenes and we thought at least we would be warm, but no, it was built in a prefabricated building with no heating. So between scenes a little warm room was found for us, and there we sat, ran our lines and talked.

I loved talking to her about the people she had worked with, especially Marlon Brando, with whom she became great friends. Stephanie told me about her daughters and her grandson. I could tell from what she said that she was the rock of her family, how much she loved them and that they were her life. I could see how strong she was, and how calm. We would all count ourselves lucky to have someone like that looking after us.

I was pleased that she could tell me about these things and the time we had together was gentle. Although we never actually talked about our mutual spiritual understanding, it was eloquently expressed.

In performance she was brilliant. Absolutely there, and all I had to do was respond. I felt totally relaxed when acting with her, enjoying her dedication, truthfulness and generosity.

Then tragedy struck. Sara, my wife, who was my rock and did everything for me, died suddenly and unexpectedly. Filming stopped and I was away for three weeks. When I came back, it was too early and I was still feeling raw, but I did not want to keep everyone waiting. At that time, in the state that I was in,

I could think of no better person to be with than Stephanie. She helped me just by her presence, and the quiet way in which we carried on with our scenes. I believe that everything is meant to be and, as Stephanie says in the book, we were there for each other in those difficult times.

Stephanie is a very spiritual person – she is psychic and knows about angels and fairies, but she is also totally grounded. She knows when and how to bring these things into the physical world to help ease the way. These are difficult things to express but she does so simply, and in a common sense way.

She writes in a clear, straightforward manner that is a delight to read. What she has to say about her life is fascinating and intriguing, and what she has to say about philosophy and spiritual matters is a lesson to us all.

When a good person writes a good book, and writes it well, we are entertained whilst receiving great truths. This is such a book.

William Roache MBE

Prologue

Having been on this planet for nearly 65 years, I want to capture in words a few morsels of a rip-roaring roller-coaster ride of a life before short-term memory loss or some other excuse stops me. Writing a book had crossed my mind briefly at the turn of the millennium. In the preceding few years my parents had grown old and died in front of my eyes. I'd become an orphan and my priorities had changed. As my mother had approached the end of her life, it became far more important for me to speak to her every day than it was to be in a hit television series. Then in 2000 I became a grandmother. I moved out of the city and back to the coast and decided finally to give up on men. I retired to the seaside and got a dog.

But the book didn't happen and I just gave up men for a while, because then I met Bernie. Perhaps I'd thought the ride was going to slow down, but it had too much momentum and happiness can arrive at any age.

During the Noughties I did some of my best theatre: *A Busy Day*, *Elizabeth Rex* and *Master Class*, all with Jonathan Church directing. I toured the UK with Simon Williams in his *Nobody's Perfect*, and Sir Peter Hall's name was on the *Hay Fever* poster but I don't think he even came to see it. I worked on four films and parts in two filmed series, and did *Bad Girls*, *Coronation Street*, *Strictly Come Dancing* and *Celebrity Big Brother*, to name just a few of the umpteen things I did for television. Not a very convincing retirement. I'm a grafter and I don't stop and probably never will. As for my poor dog, I got another one to keep her company.

I fell in love with the theatre and acting as a teenager and, nearly half a century later, the love affair continues. I still find the whole process of putting on a production fascinating. Michael Winner once said to me, 'My dear, nobody needs the film industry except the film industry.' I don't think that's true. Theatre, films, music and all the arts are capable of nourishing the soul and opening the heart. Mankind needs that food. I need that food and I feel very blessed that I've been allowed to join in and play.

Everything I've done has been of its time. It's been a magical ride that only happened because I was born when I was. The war was over. It was the perfect time to be born – when it was safe to be a child. There was an innocence and a sense of freedom. I'm a product of that age.

I could have been the poster child for the 1950s, and the 1960s pointed me towards where I am today. In the 1970s I co-starred alongside a pair of screen legends, and then got blacklisted from Hollywood. The big characters I played on screen in the 1980s were totally of their time – Connie's hot-wired living and Sable Colby's shoulder pads. In the 1990s the buck stopped with me and my life changed emphasis, but without slowing down.

On the first night my parents moved into their marital home my mother cooked a chicken. She hadn't cooked one before and she left the giblets in. The next morning she was amazed because the servants hadn't cleared it all away. It took until it happened for her to realize that she didn't have servants. Just as I was a product of my time, she was a product of hers, but liberal and progressive rather than staid and oppressed. She made me believe I could do whatever I put my mind to, and supported me throughout.

I've tried to do the same for my children, being ever aware of the difficulties they faced having a mother with a public profile. I also had to struggle with the responsibilities of being a single parent. It's directed the professional choices I've made. I know I've done less good work than I could have done. I discovered that if I was playing really big roles, I wasn't able to be a good mum. I don't mean high camp Sable Colby. That was just lipstick thick; involving fabulous bitchy lines and Oscar Wilde delivery, but it wasn't emotionally draining. It was far more difficult to combine motherhood with deep and complex characters. So for the most part I didn't play them, until after the millennium.

After I was separated from my husband, John McEnery, at the end of the 1970s, I had a choice to make. I knew I only had energy for children and work, or I could go for children, a new husband and a little bit of work here and there. I would have lost my independence. I'd put my faith in that set-up once before and it hadn't worked. So I chose to make my life without a man; determinedly independent – foolishly independent, even.

As a child my favourite Ladybird Book had been *The Sly Fox and the Little Red Hen*. Throughout my life its positive line in women's independence has inspired me: "'Then I'll do it myself," said the Little Red Hen.' I grew up with second-wave feminism. I cherish my independence. I'm of my time.

But I'm not a serious person. I'm a lightweight. I'm a jackdaw who picks up shiny stones. I'm a spiritual bungee jumper. And I've got into some sticky scrapes that have meant I've had to develop a practical set of tools to get myself off the floor whenever I've been down. Earlier in my life there was an element of 'seeking', but mainly because I had to find answers to help me solve my problems. Without the answers, and the toolkit I was able to develop with them, I would have sunk.

There have been a few moments when I've felt truly touched by God. I've seen the fabric of the universe and it's beautiful. More than anything, those moments set me on a spiritual search of greater depth. They made me realize that time is an irrelevance. I've no idea how long those moments lasted, whether minutes or seconds, but each sent ripples across the whole of my life, as if those moments have never ceased.

I'm a collector of joyful moments. The ticka-ticka ticka-ticka of a child's roller skates on paving stones is as good a mantra as any to lift the soul.

AUTOBIOGRAPHY IN FIVE CHAPTERS

1) I walk down the street.
There is a deep hole in the sidewalk.
I fall in.
I am lost… I am hopeless.
It isn't my fault.
It takes for ever to find a way out.

2) I walk down the same street.
There is a deep hole in the sidewalk.
I pretend I don't see it.
I fall in again.
I can't believe I'm in the same place.
But it isn't my fault.
It still takes a long time to get out.

3) I walk down the same street.
There's a deep hole in the sidewalk.
I see it is there.
I still fall in… it's a habit.
My eyes are open.
I know where I am.
It is my fault.
I get out immediately.

4) I walk down the same street.
There is a deep hole in the sidewalk.
I walk around it.

5) I walk down another street.

POEM FROM *THE TIBETAN BOOK OF LIVING AND DYING*

BY SOGYAL RINPOCHE

Chapter One

Many Lives

Things can happen to us in our lives that defy all logic: something in a sentence, a daydream, a vision, a visitation; it could be that you suddenly find yourself in the presence of angels. When it's happened you ask yourself how long it lasted. It could have been minutes in our linear time, or just seconds. We think in such linear terms, but we are not linear. Our lives are not linear.

Sometimes we can go through months and months, with time just passing by. Then suddenly there's a flash. The detail of those months might be lost and forgotten, but that flash will stay with us for ever.

We're so interested in time, so caught up by time. We use a linear notion of time to try to pin down the magic of existence. Time stretches and loops. Our lives stretch and loop. Our existence *is* magic.

The question that dances like a firefly in my mind is: are we following a pre-written chronicle of our lives that's unfolding as a surprise to us but that is as planned as a Disneyland ride? Or do we have free will, and a set of lessons to learn, which, if we don't get them the first time, will come back in a different form until we do?

My life has been a magic ride that could only have happened because I was born on the very day and at the very time I was. I don't think it was an accident that I was a child in the 1950s, that I *lived* the 1960s, had children in the 1970s and then came to represent, through my part in *The Colbys*, the 1980s. Are we just watching the unfurling of the inevitable or are we able to change everything, about ourselves and our future? I'm not one of the great thinkers; just someone experiencing and looking, and finding it all so incredibly interesting.

Everything in my life has been of its time. I went from a little deaf girl in Start-rite sandals in the 1950s to a voraciously inquisitive young woman in the 1960s; then from an actress and film star to a desperately struggling single mother in the 1970s. In the 1980s, the on-screen characters that I was best known for stood for that decade, while in the 1990s I went on a journey which, some years earlier, three psychics had, quite independently, told me I'd follow.

I had already started that journey way back. I don't even think it had started in this life. Like all of our lives, if you could line up each moment and look at them as if through a prism, taking them in from different perspectives, you'd see there were no contradictions; you'd see how it all connects. Just like a good haircut, everything joins up.

Angel Friends

Flying has been a theme in my life for ever. As a very young child I can remember walking along the back of the sofa and thinking that if I carried on walking I'd be able to lift off straight into the air. I believed I could fly.

The idea of having wings wasn't strange. Angels were not alien.

Every night as a child I'd go with my two angel friends and we'd fly around and do good deeds for people. They were my night-time friends: two fairy angels. We might see an old lady who needed her shopping carried, or a cat stuck in a tree that needed rescuing. We were good flying people. I thought they lived in my pillow because they came out and played when my head was resting on it.

A memory-trace carried with me into this life from before I was born, perhaps.

Mary

Being Church of England was just who we were as a family, it went with being English middle-class residents in a safe, comfortable, quiet and leafy suburb – in Barnet, North London. 'The nearest I want to get to church is the garden,' my father used to say, 'and I'm very happy to tend it.'

My mother was a spiritual person by nature. She maintained her own faith, which included a belief in an afterlife. For her, the C of E was good for christenings, funerals and weddings but it wasn't where her spirit really lay. She was far more open and investigative; spiritually restless. Unlike people who suddenly take up a definitive religious position just before death, my mother let it all unravel. When she was dying I asked her, 'Do you know where you're going next?' With a child-like twinkle in her eye, she replied, 'We'll just have to wait and see, won't we?'

Our parents sent me and my older sister Diana, who we called Didi (pronounced dye-dye), and my younger sister Jenny to a Catholic convent for our primary education. It was run by an order of French nuns. Our parents' decision to send us there was totally pragmatic. They knew we'd get the best education at the convent; at the very least, we'd learn good deportment and French.

I hated it at first; with its strict rules and regulations and a uniform that was meant to be kept neat and tidy at all times. In winter we would wear a scratchy green tunic, shirt and tie. The tunic was only cleaned once a term, and by the time the holidays began it was egg- and paint-stained. My tie would be tied just once at the start of term and then hung in a loop on the end of the bed at night, so all I had to do was slip it over my head each morning. I remember the desperately cold winters of the 1950s. So cold, we always dressed under the bedclothes. In the summer we'd change into green checked cotton dresses; our white knee-high socks held up by home-made elastic garters.

I enjoyed the religious aspects of the convent. The day was punctuated with prayer. There was chapel in the morning, prayers in between each class and at the end of the day, and we said grace before lunch. There were statues of Our Lady and of Jesus Christ throughout the school. A crucifix hung in each classroom and paintings depicting scenes from the Bible were hung on the walls. As a young child I was in awe. I took it all very seriously. I treasured my blue plastic rosary kept in a little blue egg.

During break I'd retreat to my secret places of sanctuary. In the winter months, or when it was raining, I'd slip into the little side chapel. I'd make the sign of the cross, genuflect and take my place in a front pew, then spend the rest of our 20-minute break-time praying. I didn't pray to Jesus or to God, but to the Virgin Mary.

When the weather was fine I'd skip down a path in the school's garden to a small grotto where there was another statue of Mary. I was entranced by her blue-and-white dress and the calla lilies that she held. I was drawn to her. I felt that we had a special relationship.

The Holy Trinity didn't work for me: there was a God in the clouds who spoke with a voice of anger and judgement; then there was Jesus who seemed to have a nice life but then died in agony for our sins; then there was this bird that was called a ghost that radiated light and that people wore on badges. I didn't get it. Mary wasn't angry or judgemental like God and I didn't really understand what sin was, especially mortal sin. I couldn't understand why a baby who hadn't been christened wouldn't go to heaven. The bird didn't seem like anything you would want to talk to and God seemed so fierce. Not like Mary.

In the chapel, which was a place of silence and reverence, I never spoke out loud to her, but in the garden I would. I'd chat to her about so many different things, and she'd speak to me. They weren't conversations I was having with myself in my mind. I remember them as dialogues; they were real. I talked to Mary and she talked to me. I could see and hear her. Mary was my friend and I loved her.

I didn't know why sometimes I couldn't hear things properly but I could always hear Mary. I loved the peace and calm of her grotto and the chapel; away from the babble and confusing noise of the playground.

The nuns had noticed that I spent a lot of time in the chapel or down the end of the garden in Mary's alcove. Late one afternoon, after I'd got home from school, my mother received a telephone call from one of the Sisters suggesting, in a softly spoken and gentle way, that they believed I'd be a good candidate for conversion. I think my mother was a little surprised. She was aware that I'd shown an interest in religion but thought it was just a passing phase. She also knew that the nuns were always on the look-out for new recruits and wasn't at all comfortable with the idea of me being corralled into committing to a faith I knew little about. Far too elegant ever to offend anyone, however, and also of the belief that you should never argue with those of the cloth, especially nuns, my mother listened till the Sister had finished, then simply said, 'That sounds just lovely, Sister, and I expect that you are right, and if Stephie does want to pursue this when she is a little older then that would be simply wonderful!'

They didn't call again.

Curiosity Saved This Cat

When I was a teenager I was out most evenings. On Mondays I'd go to the church youth club and jive to Everly Brothers' and Bobby Darin records. On Tuesday evenings we'd all meet at the Black Horse pub and then go to Barnet Jazz Club, where they had live music and we could spend the evening long-arm jiving to Acker Bilk and other traditional jazz bands. On Wednesdays we'd head to the further education college for more dancing, and come Friday we'd be at the Finchley Jazz Club for short-arm jiving. The only night I didn't go out was Thursday. I stayed in to wash my hair. Saturday morning it was up the Devon Café, at the far end of Barnet High Street, to find out where the party was Saturday night. On Sunday afternoons I would spread all my books out over the dining room table and do my homework for the complete week while listening to Radio Luxembourg.

When Geoff, my first boyfriend, came along, I calmed down; my parents saw the advantage. My reports improved, I started to read and develop an interest in culture and art; if only, at first, to be able to keep up with Geoff in conversation. Geoff and his friends opened my mind to a whole new realm of concepts and ideas and I was there, absorbing it all. I was learning from them all the time: what to read, what to question and what to think. In many ways my relationship with Geoff was as much an education as it was a romance. He and his friends fed my hunger for knowledge. I was very lucky; I wanted to learn. I wanted to know everything. It was just what I needed.

Things do seem to happen at the right time.

New words like 'hypotheses', 'philosophy', 'agnostic' and 'atheist' came into my vocabulary. Suddenly, talking to… wait a minute? The Virgin Mary? Put those childish things behind you and think about 'logic'. If you can't see it – does it exist? Reading about Lenin, Stalin, Mao Tse-tung; discovering that there were societies which had abandoned religion for ideologies of human communalism. I was ready to challenge everything, and I wasn't afraid of anything. Searching, questioning, examining; I had no fear in rejecting what had gone before.

My Versailles

At the age of five I won a fancy dress competition playing a Spanish señorita. Someone put a fan in my hand. It felt as if it was an extension of my hand and completely natural. I knew exactly how to use it. Some people can hold a musical instrument and feel its essence, its inner quality; whenever I held a fan I could tell if it was weighted properly – whether it was good or not. I have always known the art and language of the fan. It's a very slight talent, but it is mine. Where did it come from?

When I was 13 I spent the summer in France with Geoff and a group of his friends. It was 1960. We'd hitchhiked down from Calais to the Côte d'Azur and spent five glorious weeks on the beaches of the Riviera in a world so far removed from dowdy postwar England. When our money ran out and the summer was drawing to a close, we headed back to Calais. En route we stopped off at Versailles.

One of the largest palaces in the world, I was immediately struck by its scale, beauty and grandeur. At the same time, it wasn't unfamiliar. Reaching the entrance to the magnificent gardens, which led to the palace itself, I broke away from the others and began to explore on my own.

As I made my way along the main walkway, past the fountains and avenues of trees, I could see groups of tourists following a circuit around the gardens and into the palace. I began to follow them, and found myself going in another direction, along a wall surrounding an ornamental garden to the right of the main palace building. I wasn't sure why I was heading that way, I just seemed to be drawn in that direction. As I approached an archway

Fan work on the phone – appearing in The Rover *with the RSC (1988)*

leading into the garden a guard halted me in my tracks, holding up a hand to stop me from passing.

'*Vous ne pouvez passer par là!*' He said officiously, blocking my way.

Without thinking, I replied, '*Mais je prends toujours cette route.*'

The words 'But I always go this way' just fell out of my mouth. I've no idea where they came from. The guard gave me an incredulous look as if to say 'Who on Earth do you think you are?' I turned and walked away. Rather than head back to the front of the palace building, though, I found myself retreating back to the garden, but this time by another route. I wasn't sure what I was doing or where I was going. For some reason I felt I had to be there.

This time there wasn't anyone to stop me. As I walked into the garden I noticed a side entrance to the palace. The door was open so I went inside. I noticed the floor of the room I'd stepped into. It looked remarkably old and worn to me. I was alone in the room and, as I took in my surroundings, my eyes were drawn to the bust of a man resting on a cabinet. It was a very modest figure of a naval officer. I felt the colour rise to my cheeks as I looked at it. I felt an overwhelming sense of connection to the man that the figure depicted. I knew this man. I didn't know his name and I also didn't know how I knew he was an officer in the King's Navy. What I did know was that I had loved that man.

Surprised and taken aback by the strength of the feelings and thoughts that had surged up inside me, I stepped outside again. Standing on the gravel path, I thought I'd head back to the main garden and look for the others. All at once I found myself looking up towards a window on the third floor. 'That's where I used to be,' I thought. 'That's where I was. I used to live here.'

Images started to tumble into my mind and in a flash my awareness shifted and I was no longer there in the present day but in another time, and as another person. I was a member of the court of the King during the *ancien régime*. I wasn't part of the inner circle of servants and maids-in-waiting but for some reason had been sneaked into the King's apartments to watch his *petit lever*. I'm not sure in what capacity I was part of the court but there had been an occasion when I had been part of the select few who watched the ceremonial custom of the King waking and dressing in the morning. I'd seen him stretching and yawning and going about his *toilette*. I had been there.

The vision passed. I looked around. I was standing alone by the door I'd gone through, hearing a murmur of visitors' voices coming from the front of the palace. I made my way back around the building and began scanning the groups of people for Geoff and the others. As I stood there, calmly looking for my friends, I felt my awareness changing again. Looking at the magnificent palace in front of me, my sight began to blur and a new set of images began to form in my line of vision.

I could see myself sitting at a rickety table in a wood-panelled room, playing cards with a group of gentlemen. The cards are long and thin and rather unusual-looking. The room is filled with a dusty light and the smell of sweat, pomade, body odour and cologne. I'm in my early twenties, delicately powdered and wearing a slightly worn, faded pink brocade. The men I'm playing with are engaged in a philosophical debate that I'm listening to but not expected to take part in. There's a small, thick drinking glass on the table; blown rather than cut, and with tiny bubbles in the glass. Around me I can see people with powdered wigs and walking sticks, and women with fans showing cleavage. I'm not wearing a wig and I'm aware that my dusky pink dress isn't as fine as the dresses worn by the other women in the room. I'm neither a servant nor a whore, but I'm not very high up on the social ladder. I'm some kind of courtesan; a girl brought into the salon to entertain gentlemen, play cards, enjoy a glass of wine with them, and flirt a little. The whole scene is pervaded by a relaxed atmosphere, with an air of genteel entertainment and pleasure. A door opens to my left, through which a grand and glamorous, tightly-corseted and white-wigged lady enters. That's where the vision ended.

I can't say how long it lasted; maybe it was just seconds, a matter of minutes, or maybe longer. All I knew was that what I had seen was as real as the world I came back to. I had been there, in that salon. Whether or not it was the same person who witnessed the King's *petit lever*, I have no idea.

The thing about these moments is that they usually come complete in themselves, and without answers. Yet somehow they are answers in themselves: answers to questions that run through our lives that are sometimes as trivial-seeming as why a five-year-old girl would know how to wield a fan, perfectly. And of course, the floor of the room with the bust looked rather sad and old and worn in 1960, compared to how it would have looked 300 years earlier.

The amazing thing was, from that moment I instinctively knew information and facts about French history from that period. When I heard it, the name Madame de Rambouillet was immediately familiar. I knew she had been the woman that had walked into the room at the end of my vision. It was in her salon that I had been playing cards.

Some time later, after a French history test at school, my teacher came up to me. 'How did you do so well?' she asked. 'I know you did absolutely *no* revision.'

'I didn't need to,' I replied. 'I already knew it.'

Inevitabilities

Things often happen when you least expect them, catching you totally unprepared. They can be a bit shocking. I call them *inevitabilities*.

April 1991, six o'clock in the morning; I'd just arrived to work at a studio in Los Angeles. Walking across the parking lot my eyes suddenly met those of a guy dragging cables across the tarmac. In an instant we both knew we had to talk to each other. A spontaneous wave passed between us and there and then we gave each other a hug. It was like a lightning strike; a bolt of energy between us that came as if from nowhere. I could see he'd been totally shocked. Nothing like this had ever happened to him before.

We met later and I asked him what he'd felt. 'Relief,' he said. 'In the instant we saw each other I thought, "there she is".'

I later discovered he was a cameraman-director, but that day he was working on an infomercial for a friend. What he'd felt, and seen, completely corresponded with what I had.

'We were children,' he continued. 'We were a little boy and girl running down a hill. There were windmills in the background.

We're dressed in old-fashioned clothes. There's a carriage and we're parted and the wheels are very big. We never see each other again.'

It was exactly what I'd seen: the scene was 17th-century Flemish, and the carriage's wheels would have seemed big – we were children. I looked at him. 'And now, here we are… '

It led to three years together and a lifelong friendship.

I know that we come in and out of each other's lives across incarnations, and sometimes when we meet people again who we've known in a previous life, we go through the opposite relationship dynamic with them. You might meet the same soul again that you've had a relationship with in a past life but you may well not have the same relationship with them this time around. Sometimes you might be drawn together again to pass on, or receive, a message.

A few years ago I met a man at a friend's party. I didn't find him attractive but I knew there was some kind of connection between us that I had to explore. I found him perfectly amicable and felt comfortable in his company, and over the period of a few weeks we went out together a couple of times and started to get to know each other. During one of our dates I suddenly had a vision. When I experience these visions, although it appears out of focus I can still see the room I'm in or wherever I happen to be, but the vision is completely there in front of my eyes, like it was in Versailles.

My vision was of a sweet working-class couple on a tandem bicycle in a country setting, arriving at their destination and then having a picnic. The boy was dressed up in a brown suit and wearing a cap. The girl was wearing a pale blouse and a long skirt, slightly hitched up. The historical setting was pre-First World War. I have no idea if people rode tandem bicycles then but that's what I saw them on. Their picnic was modest but full. They had little pieces of cotton with beads covering their food dishes.

Dramatically and violently I'm pulled out of that scene and thrown into the trenches during the First World War. I can see dressed legs and bits of body flying through the air and blood spattering. The boy who had been on the picnic is there; covered in blood, in anguish and totally disillusioned. He's about to die.

So, there I am, having this terrifying vision. I'm huddled in a corner, frightened. I'm in war. I'm in the trenches. I'm weeping. I say to the man I've had a few dates with: 'You don't have to be here any more. You must know that in this life you don't need to be frightened. It won't happen to you again.'

I have no idea what happened to the girl. I assume I was her, but I didn't 'get' her – I got the boy. To the best of my knowledge the man I was with had been the boy I'd seen in the vision, who had died in the trenches in the First World War.

It was as if I was the messenger from his guardian angels sent to tell him that he didn't need to be afraid any more. He'd carried that sense of terror with him from that incarnation and it continued to disable him. He was being haunted by a basic fear of everything. I had to tell him it wasn't real; that it was from a life before this one and that he should drop it.

For me, the amazing thing was that after that there was absolutely no chemistry between us. For him, I was completely insane. He thought I was frightful, but I didn't feel responsible for how he felt. Our connection was about the message I had to give him.

From the moment we met I knew there was something between us; I just didn't know what it was, and I had no idea it was going to happen like it did. I knew our connection wasn't on the level of an intimate relationship but I had to follow my feeling, in the same way that I had to follow whatever it was that led me to that room in Versailles. I just needed to give him the message that he need no longer be permanently suspicious and frightened.

For some reason I'd never been to Egypt. Something had stopped me from going – a feeling inside. I hadn't wanted to go. When I eventually went with my friend Lisa Voice, I really felt nothing for the pyramids, but when I saw the temple of Abu Simbel in southern Egypt, even though it had been displaced – moved from its original location when the Aswan Dam was built – I immediately felt at home. I wasn't a Cairo kid or a Luxor baby; I was from the outer territories. When I looked at them, the hieroglyphs didn't seem alien. I'm never going to be able to translate the Rosetta Stone, but I could read them. They made sense to me.

It is thoroughly disappointing that I wasn't Cleopatra. All I can say about my Egyptian incarnation is that it was lowly and fearful. Unlike other incarnations, I have no sense of detail, just a sense of wariness about it. The only thing I feel is that I was an Israelite, in Egypt as a slave.

My having resisted going to Egypt before, despite having had plenty of opportunities, suddenly made sense. Particular people and specific places resonate with us as echoes across our many lives.

Lisa Voice and me in Egypt

The Answers Are in Our Pasts

When I was 36 I 'died' and was brought back. The experience was profound. It changed the course of my life. Up until then it had been a head-on rush: a brazen and fearless adventure in which I'd gone from the highest of highs to the lowest of lows and back again; powered by adrenaline, sheer will, focused intention and hard work. From my earliest childhood I'd launched myself headlong into the wonder of life's possibilities, and up to the point of my near-death I'd been physically driven. If there was a wall to climb or a window to climb out of, I was onto or out of it. As a teenager I just upped the pace and by the time I was carving out a successful career as an actress in my twenties and thirties I was skiing down mountainsides, leaping off cliffs, diving, running, jumping; all the time thinking, 'If I die now I'll die having the most fun.' And then I did die.

After my near-death I went to see three psychics. Each of them told me the same thing: that up to that point I'd been living very much on the physical plane but the second half of my life would be far more focused on the spiritual. I took what they said; particularly since each one had given me the same message but, at the time, I didn't know how it would pan out.

Not so many years later, what they'd said all began to fall into place.

I went to Hollywood in 1985 and was very soon on the spiritual journey they'd described, but I felt frustrated with myself. I didn't seem to be able to find a spiritual home; somewhere I could settle. I couldn't understand why I seemed to be such a dipper and diver, so I went to see Dr Ron Scolastico, a spiritual counsellor. Entering a deep trance state Ron accessed what he called The Guides. Before going into trance he'd told me to think about the question I'd come to him with, and not to tell him what it was but to keep it in the front of my mind. He began speaking in a very odd voice and, as I later said to myself, if I'd just spent $75 watching someone act it was money well spent because he kept it up for well over an hour. I don't think he was acting, though. I genuinely believe that he was channelling – that his Guide was speaking through him. He had absolutely no idea of my question but the answer I got from his Guide was bang-on-centre-target.

Ron's Guide described a tall and gaunt woman living in Roman times in the latter years of her life. She had a high social status and had lived well and comfortably. Coming to the end of her days, her entire life had been dedicated to worshipping various gods. But a deep sense of regret pervaded her spirit because she'd realized that her life's dedication had been to false gods.

I have no doubt that Ron's Guide described a past incarnation of mine; one that the second half of the incarnation I'm in now will resolve. The message I received was that this half of my life would be about my finding my own belief system. It didn't contradict anything that I'd been told before; it just affirmed what I was doing. It wasn't as if there were mixed messages coming from the other side so it made me feel good. It made me realize that I have spiritual purpose – I just don't have spiritual form. After that I was able to put my jackdaw's approach into a context that went beyond this life, and I stopped worrying about it.

I'm a spiritual bungee jumper. A jackdaw, collecting brightly coloured stones in a deep, medieval suede bag. It's my way.

Friends and Other Relations

My best friend Colin and I have accepted that we've been in and out of each other's lives so many times that we don't bother to think about it any more. It's just a given. In one life or other we've been in every relationship possible. Like with the man who was in my vision of the trenches, when I met Colin I felt no attraction towards him whatsoever on an intimate level; and he the same towards me. Unlike the other man, with Colin the connection wasn't immediate. Different recipes require a different setting on the cooking timer.

I'd already been living in California for a few years when I met Colin – set up on a blind date with him by mutual friends. We were both free and single and, when our friends put two and two together, on paper at least we seemed to be the ideal match. But we were instantaneously apathetic towards each other. There was no way I was even vaguely interested, and I'm sure he felt the same. My daughters Phoebe and Chloe, however, were very keen on the idea of Colin, especially Chloe, since she'd heard that he kept horses. To her, the fact that he had 17 of them made him the most eligible man on the planet.

'Go on three dates with him at least, and after that if you can't do kissing you can start seeing other people, but you have to have three proper dates first,' they insisted. 'With lipstick on, Mummy!'

So Colin and I went out three times but there was no kissing and, rather than dating Colin, I started seeing the seemingly unsuitable young man I'd met in the studio parking lot. Our lives are the way they're meant to be.

Jude

Similar to the way Colin and I have cropped up in each other's lives across many incarnations, I know it's been the same with my grandson Jude. There was a time when I really wondered what my relationship with Jude should be. I loved him so deeply, as I'm sure every grandmother loves their grandchild, but he was also in a precarious situation because my daughter Phoebe and his father were divorcing. I wanted to know what my position should be in the midst of it all.

During a past-life regression I got that I was standing outside a tepee. My feet were hurt; I'd been on burnt ground. I was Native American and there was an attack coming. Everybody had to leave, but I was an old woman with damaged feet and I knew that I couldn't go as I would have held the others up.

One of the young warriors rode up and acknowledged me. 'You have done good work,' he said. 'You are a good person. I see you. I appreciate you.' It was enough for me. The young warrior was Jude. He had seen me and that is all I am meant to do for Jude in this life: see him and make sure he feels acknowledged and recognized for who he is. Maybe that's all a grandmother is meant to do anyway.

My life and Jude's have intersected in other incarnations, but this is the most important realization for our lives now. All I have to do is make sure he knows he is truly seen as himself, that he also knows he is truly loved, and that I'm always here for him.

During this past-life regression, I also experienced the old woman's death:

I get a wound in my side. The others have left and there are people, other Native Americans, attacking. Some are wearing

Jude and me, photographed by Judy Geeson

navy blue cavalry uniform dress coats; maybe there are white men, too, but I can't see any. I'm aware of charred ground, a battle, blood, a wound in my side, a spear; I'm in pain, it's awful, then I can no longer feel any pain.

I'm rising up like a figure in a painting by Chagall; being drawn back inside the tepee I'd been standing outside but rising up towards its apex. I rise through the top of the tepee and pass Buffalo, Fox and Wolf and all the totem animals, and then further up through something that's like a chimney. I'm no longer old. I'm just hanging in space and young. Then upwards again, and I'm in a flawless scene: two black-and-white pinto ponies are peacefully grazing on lush green grass close to a perfect wigwam. Above me, puffy white clouds hang in a blue crystal sky. I look down at my immaculate moccasins. I have black plaits with beads. My partner is on the horizon. I realize I'm in the Happy Hunting Ground because I've died the death that I would have expected, being that person, and gone where she would have expected to go. As soon as I realize this, the scene begins to dissolve.

And it's OK that it melts away. It's lovely but we don't need that. Now I'm simply in the Presence. There is great belief: perfection that no words can really describe.

And there's golden light, but solid like a huge curtain. Every single cell is shining and shimmering and being renewed. Every bit of light is individual but all in the same mass. You might see it as sinewy, or like a cape made up of strands of really soft, pure gold thread – each like the double helix of DNA, with energy of golden light secured to it.

It's the soul bank, where our spirits return after passing for cleansing, renewing and restoring: a total meltdown of everything;

yet it's not a meltdown. I can't tell you what it is. Little wonder gold has deep spiritual significance: refined gold ore as the earthly representation of the heavenly golden light.

Then I think: there's so much free will in life, I thought it was going to be limited by *rules*. In answer a Pegasus – a white horse with enormous white wings – appears before me and tells me:

> *I wrap you in the blanket of love*
> *But I will not bind you with the comfort or*
>   *constraints of obligation.*
> *You might be glad to begin a task but the real truth is*
>   *you don't* have *to do anything,*
> *And you are allowed to choose.*
> *The only absolute is that love comes to you, and is*
>   *the only motivator*
> *If it's not motivated by love – what's the point?*

Everybody comes to the same conclusion – there is only love. There is only love… or fear. At the end of your life you get the scene, images and people that mirror your background and expectations. We get the death we expect. Surely that's where heaven and hell come from. If you've been a bad person you'll have a terrible time. You create your own heaven or hell. We go to the energy we know. I know, because I died in this life… and then I came back. More about that later.

When we stop looking for the logic in things, we open the door to the fantastic and magical. Miracles will follow close behind.

Chapter Two

A Moment of Knowing

When I was 19 I had an epiphany, a profound experience that came completely out of the blue.

I was at RADA – the Royal Academy of Dramatic Art – *the* most prestigious place to study acting. Back then only one in 200 girls was accepted each term, and on top of that I was awarded a scholarship. The gods were already holding my hand.

RADA was vibrant, busy, demanding and thoroughly challenging. I knew I was really lucky – I'd found what I wanted to do with my life and I'd landed in the best place to do it. I was completely immersed. Mime, music, dance, speech, diction, fencing, studying playwrights – and balancing a budget. I could afford either a lipstick or cigarettes or lunch. On the days I chose lunch, to save time I used to pour soup on top of mashed potato on top of a salad, gobble it up and get back to studying. I never drank and I didn't know of the existence of drugs. My life was down to earth and full.

One day, hot, sweaty and in my leotard, having just finished a movement class, I went up to the roof for some fresh air before voice class. It was an ordinary day of back-to-back classes, enjoyable but nothing special.

I was on the roof in the sunshine, when suddenly from nowhere I was overcome with the most overwhelming and all-encompassing sense of such sweetened joy and peace. It shimmered towards me as a wave. Everything around me became brilliant and beautiful. It was a feeling of such heightened intensity that it took my breath away. I was elated. I felt euphoric.

With this feeling of ultimate peace and joy came a sense of *knowing*. A deep understanding that everything was one, and that I was an intrinsic part of all that is. I was not separate from the world. I was not separate from the whole universe.

I had no sense of difference, no feeling of being apart from anything. The molecular form of my body and the molecular make-up of everything around me, and of the whole universe, was all the same. I was connected to everything and, in turn, everything was connected to me.

And there was life in *everything*: the ladders on the roof, my handbag, the ground I was standing on, the windows of the buildings I could see across the street – those supposedly inanimate objects were alive and I could *feel* their vibrancy. I could *feel* the molecules moving in my shoes. *Everything* around me vibrated with life.

As this wave of understanding washed over me I gave up the sense of my own self to a greater force. I was still present, I could still see and feel myself, but I was conscious that who *I* was, wasn't the body I was in; this vessel of blood and bones. *I* was the life that was within me. It flowed through my soul, and it reflected my soul everywhere and in everything.

I was one with the entire universe, and limitless. In that instant, I realized I wasn't a separate entity but part of the whole. I was important, but no more important than anyone or anything else. I was just a tiny speck in the vast totality of the universe, but deeply woven into its fabric, and I realized that my life had purpose.

I knew the mystery and miracle of life itself, of how everything was interconnected. The air that I breathed, the ground beneath me, the trees in the distance, the people on the street below; absolutely nothing existed in isolation – everything joined up.

The joy and the peace were *so* intense – so palpable. I just let it all flow through me and fill me up. I had been touched by a divine wand and I felt blessed – truly blessed. God, the *absolute* truth of the universe, blasted through my every cell. I saw a beauty in life that I had never seen before. I felt a sense of peace that I had never known before. My heart was filled with the greatest joy and I didn't want it to end.

In the miracle of that moment I saw perfection in all things. In that moment I was allowed to rest because I was part of that perfection. I'd arrived; the search was over. I felt a sense of total relief.

I can't say how long it lasted.

That experience had the most profound impact on me. Why had I been given this gift? Is the universe random in its munificence? Where had it come from? Ever since then, I have been left with a huge feeling of gratitude, and an unrelenting longing.

I had glimpsed the presence of God – I didn't make it to voice class.

Nearly 50 years later, the memory of that moment on the rooftop at RADA remains pure and intact. To me it is, and always has been, completely moving, because it is *the* answer. It's what you search your whole life to understand: the *fabric* of everything is the same.

You can be told this, but you don't really believe it. Just as you don't really believe that the molecules that make up matter are moving. It's something you're told. You understand it as a concept, intellectually – but when you experience it, you're beyond words. For the first time I can see you as you are, because you are me and I am you. Suddenly I can touch you; I can feel all things, and all at once. There are no divisions between us.

Since then, I've understood emotionally that there is no contradiction between the findings of quantum physics and the Hindu Upanishads. For that short space of time, all was opened up to me. It was on the level of the soul bank of cleansing, renewing and restoring; of the golden threads of DNA. It was the tapestry of the universe, the essence of what we are beyond this mortal coil – pure spirit.

I believe a time will come when physicists are able to weigh the soul. Is the body a whisper lighter after its last breath; exited by a departing physicality that we don't understand? Like dark matter in the universe: totally unseen, yet its effects apparent. Like the neutrino, hurtling from the sun to pass undetected through our bodies and on through the Earth, observable only through the effects of its impact on other particles in cathedral-sized detectors. The soul is there in the geometry of the fractal-like golden matter of the universe; known but not always acknowledged.

Ever since, I've been a starer at sunsets and sunrises; wistful for that moment of knowing.

Sunset on the beach with Nutrina and Sienna

Chapter Three

Theatre

In the Beginning

My first two appearances on stage could have put me off acting for life and, ever since, I've probably just being trying to make up for them.

Out of all the children in school I was specially selected to present our Reverend Mother with a posy of flowers at a farewell ceremony before she left for a sabbatical in France. During the ceremony I had to climb the stairs to the stage with the posy, make my way to where she was sitting and, having presented the flowers to her with a little curtsey, bid her *bon voyage*. How hard could that be?

Well, quite hard when you're only four years old, actually. Trying to retain two words of French when you're that small is like having to learn the entire canon of Shakespeare, and it really didn't help that said posy was not a posy at all but a bunch of gladioli that matched me in height. I got rather fussed about the whole thing. It wasn't helped by the fact that Didi and all her 'big girl' friends were watching me and smirking. Under the weight of all the flowers I tripped on the stairs and, by the time I reached Reverend Mother's chair, I'd forgotten my line. I promptly burst into tears in front of the whole school and hid in her voluminous black skirts. Let's just say it wasn't one of my finest moments on stage.

The next ghastliness was playing Chanticleer the cock, a minor role in the nativity play. My mother had sewn a jagged bit of red felt onto a balaclava to represent wattles. The felt flopped over and the hat was so big I couldn't see properly. Maybe that's the reason I've been so fussy about my costumes ever since. There were no floppy wattles for Sable.

I think I was 12 when I conned my way into the National Youth Theatre. My friend Roz and I went for an interview in one of the big white houses in Eccleston Square, near Victoria Station in London. It was number 22. I can't remember exactly how old I was, but I remember the address. Funny, the things we remember. We said we were 15 and I got in, Roz didn't. She said her favourite actor was Alfred Findley; I managed to remember his name was Albert Finney. They said I was too late to audition for an acting job so would I like to do admin or elecs? Since I hadn't a clue what either of those was, I plumped for elecs and hoped for the best. I got a job helping work the electrics board at the Scala Theatre for the summer. Left in charge for five minutes, I managed to fuse the board and cause a blackout in the middle of a scene from *Richard III* when a blackout wasn't needed. Neil Stacey was playing Richard and I had a crush on him. He was very kind about the blackout; it was the only time he spoke to me.

That wonderful actor Kenneth Cranham was friendlier and used to share his sandwiches with me. Years later, in 1979, we'd

Me as Electra – glad I wasn't playing the boy

do *The London Cuckolds* together at The Royal Court Theatre. We were also at RADA at the same time – he was in the year above me. We had supper together a few months ago when we happened to be in the same city. It's good to know people for over 50 years.

I only performed in one school play: Sophocles' *Electra*. Miss Iliff was in charge of Drama. Her brother Noel taught me radio technique at RADA. They probably came from a theatre background. I was offered the part of Chrysothemis but I didn't want to do that. 'What's the name of the play?' I asked. '*Electra*? I'll do that then.' Hey, if I was going to have to stay in after school and not get to go out dancing I might as well play the big part. I got it, and became obsessed with the role: her plight, her revenge, the tragedy. I should have known then that I'd become an actress.

My sister Didi says she's still waiting for me to do something better.

I left school after taking only Art and English A Levels, and went to Paris to study mime with Etienne Decroux. Decroux had taught Marcel Marceau, but if you asked him about Marceau, Decroux would just pull a long face and say, '*Il est mort; il n'existe plus*' – 'he is dead; he no longer exists.' This was because Marceau had used props and had become what Decroux considered commercial. Serious stuff this mime business. I was entranced for a few weeks.

While in Paris I supported myself by working as an au pair, but the family's maid took a dislike to me. Quite rightly: I was a terrible au pair. One day she threw a boot at my head and I was given a lot of Chanel No. 5 and sent back to England.

I went up to Liverpool to visit my boyfriend at the time. He'd just got a job with the newly established Liverpool Everyman. It was 1964 and Liverpool was happening. The city was alive. It was far more exciting than anywhere else. The Beatles were just one of many bands who, along with singers and beat poets, had made the city into what the poet Allen Ginsberg thought was the centre of the creative universe.

When I arrived, the company's directors, Terry Hands and Peter James, were auditioning for Carlo Goldoni's 1743 play, *The Servant of Two Masters*. It just so happened they were looking for a juvenile lead. I still remembered a Juliet monologue from *Romeo and Juliet*. I'd learned it for my English O Level.

At every stage of my life I've found myself in the right place at the right time – always at the centre of where the energy of the moment was percolating. Without any acting training I auditioned for the part – and got it.

I fell in love with theatre; my passion and openness for

learning carried me. I learned on the job – from Terry and Peter, and from the rest of the company.

As well as *The Servant of Two Masters*, we were doing Shakespeare's *Henry IV Parts 1 and 2* and *Macbeth*, and Kenneth Grahame's *Toad of Toad Hall*. It was the start of my career as an actress. In a review in the *Liverpool Echo* I was called 'the girl with the golden glow'.

I've treasured that review ever since.

I'd been in Liverpool for nearly a year when Terry decided not to cast me for their next production, Oscar Wilde's *The Importance of Being Earnest*. He said I didn't have the technique to do Wilde. I'd learned as much as I could with the company, and gone as far as I was able. Terry suggested I audition for RADA. It just so happened that John Fernald, RADA's Principal, was visiting the Everyman. After he had seen the show that night, Fernald asked me: 'What have you done before?'

'Nothing,' I replied.

'What are you going to do next?'

'Terry says I need technique and should go to RADA.'

'Then you had better come down and see me,' he said, looking over at Terry.

I did.

Being a student at RADA in the Sixties was a perfect time to be there. The world of theatre was going through a phase of growth and change. When we weren't making it ourselves, or talking about it, we were going to see it. I was passionate about the theatre. I went to see anything I could. There was so much innovation. Through his Poor Theatre – and Theatre Laboratory – Polish director Jerzy Grotowski was revolutionizing the way people looked at, thought about and experienced theatre. I managed to get a ticket for a Grotowski production, on one of the rare occasions that he was actually in England, and turned up at the venue only to be led to a van and then taken on a magical mystery tour. Eventually we were taken to a basement where we sat, very uncomfortably, for three hours of Shakespeare in Polish. I also remember being amazed by it.

Closer to home, the British director Peter Brook was experimenting with using improvisation to create theatre in innovative ways. I remember, one evening, participating in an event he led at the Roundhouse in Camden Town. Audience participation has never been high on my list of comfortable activities, but it was exciting nonetheless. Experimental theatre was high art and a must-do for a drama student, as was queuing all night for tickets for Olivier's *Othello* when the National Theatre was at the Old Vic. There were a lot of great actors and great theatre. I remember being entranced by Geraldine McEwan in Georges Feydeau's *A Flea in Her Ear*.

The theatre's a sacred place for me; it always has been, and it's never stopped pulling me back for more. It had been its theatre of rituals that had drawn me to Catholicism when I was a child. There's little glamour involved in performing in the theatre, though. It's hard work – and touring with a play is the hardest work of the lot.

I get nostalgic remembering the way theatres used to smell – greasepaint, sweat, cheap disinfectant and dust. The smell I miss most is size. It was used to prime canvas backdrops before painting. Fresh size meant fresh backdrops, a new production and an opening night; good luck cards slipped under dressing room doors, nerves and last-minute adjustments. Actors' sweat has a sharp smell: adrenaline. Adrenaline's very strong and addictive. I keep being drawn back for more.

The Harsh Reality

There's something quite stressful about Mondays on tour. First of all you have to find the theatre. I don't know why actors are always trusted to turn up. I've always envied pop stars their tour buses, and love the way a car arrives for you when you're working on a film. In theatre there's no such luck – you spend a lot of time buying train tickets and studying Google Maps. You go in and do a sound check, have a try out and a walk through – you familiarize yourself with the stage. Then I prepare my dressing room. I have a collection of sentimental things that I always put in my dressing room. There's a beautiful lace pillow case that I lay my make-up out on and there's my dressing gown. It's seen so many productions it's nearly falling apart, but I won't throw it away; it's my lucky dressing gown – we're a very superstitious bunch, us theatre folk.

Once my little home is set up I make sure I know my route to the stage. I'll make sure my props have been laid out on the props table and that my wardrobe is where it's easiest for any quick changes. It's a new space so there's a lot of organizing and finding out to be done. Then we get to do the show. After that we usually meet 'Friends of the Theatre'. Then suddenly you're alone. You haven't been to your digs. You probably don't know where they are. You're all by yourself. You haven't got water, you haven't got flowers, and you haven't sorted out anything to eat. Grabbing the sandwich left over from tea time, with too many bags in your hand you click off the light with your elbow, close the dressing room door and go off into the night. There's no glamour and it's not much fun after the show on a Monday.

Chances are on Tuesday morning you'll wake after having had a rotten night's sleep because by the time you got to your digs you couldn't work out how to operate the heating and hot water. I always travel with a hot water bottle when it's cold, in case I can't sort out the heating. I prefer to be self-catering and not stay in a hotel. If you're in a hotel the restaurant will be closed by the time you get back and the most you would be able to do is charm the porter into rustling you up a sandwich – another sandwich.

On Tuesday, if your name is above the title on the poster you're probably up bright and early to do a local radio show – because the circus is in town and you're part of the elephants' parade. It's certainly not all free time and just the show in the evening. You're probably going to have to do an interview for the local paper for next week's theatre and then you might have a little bit of rehearsing to do, as last night's show didn't go quite right. There was a hitch on your entrance when the door stuck because the stage is on a different rake and the set had gone up just before the show, as if by magic.

One of the best tours I ever did was in the Middle and Far East for the British Council. I was playing Olivia in *Twelfth Night*; Judy Geeson was playing Viola. They're not huge roles so we got to do a lot of sightseeing. Imagine playing Shakespeare to Tibetan refugees in Kathmandu. They didn't understand a word and laughed in all the wrong places. It was a lot of fun. I'm told

With Judy Geeson, rehearsing Twelfth Night

My dressing room table at the end of a week

I'm the only person ever to have asked to plug in their heated hair-rollers in Kathmandu.

Sometimes the matinee will be on a Wednesday, which means you haven't yet had time to take a breath. I love matinee audiences. They're usually old and, I always say, a standing ovation from an older audience is when they clap with their hands higher than their hearts. They've seen all the touring plays and are the most theatrically educated audience of the week. I really appreciate the effort made to get the bus, struggle through town and turn up.

On Thursday you might get to the cathedral or to the local art gallery. Chances are, though, you've got to do some repair work on yourself or buy new tights, get your nails done, get your hair washed or whatever it is that needs doing.

By Friday night it feels like you've been living in your digs for a year. I call Fridays 'Reluctant Husbands' Night'. It takes a lot of energy to keep those poor men interested, or even awake, after a long week at the office.

Saturday morning you have to pack up and get straight to your next digs by lunchtime to get to the theatre for the matinee – putting your suitcase, to carry on to the next venue, wherever the company manager tells you to. The two shows on a Saturday fly by and are generally fabulous fun. You know the theatre, you know the backstage crew and you know where the microwave is for a snack between shows. By Saturday you own the space. The dressing room you've taken over, which looks as if you've been living there for a year, has to be packed up during the show. By Saturday night when you leave the theatre, giving in your tenner to say 'thanks' to the man on the stage door for being nice, you're very tired. Depending on whether you have a long way to go, and if it involves travelling from Edinburgh down to Brighton, you might not get Sunday at home. You might have to go straight in and do digs, or you might just manage to get home and push your front door against a pile of mail.

It's hard and lonely work. A famous drummer friend of mine used to say he got paid to tour and did the drumming for free. I feel the same about my work – it's got enormous highs but, along with those, corresponding troughs. My life's been like that, too, and I feel blessed.

Rituals

I love rehearsals. They're an opportunity for a special kind of playing. It's when everything's a possibility. Ritual and theatre go hand in hand. Playing is the ritual of the imagination.

When I come into the theatre before a performance I have a ritual for settling myself in and leaving the energy of the day behind me. I wander around in ever-decreasing circles; greeting people, doing what needs doing, sorting what needs sorting, round and round until I'm by myself in my dressing room. Just like a dog does before it can lie down. It takes me time to shake off the day. I can only get into character if I get rid of my day and get rid of me.

The sacred moment of opening a new script is a ritual, too. A new script really shouldn't be flicked through for the first time on a bus or the Tube. Of course, later it's going to be in my handbag and constantly rustled with, but the first reading is very important. That is, until you get to episode 147. At that point you just flick through the pages, saying 'bullshit, bullshit, bullshit – oh, my bit…'

Some jobs you take for one reason and then you suddenly get involved with the whole thing on a different level and another reason emerges. I've made a few pretty dire films, but I got to go to Budapest, I got to live in Paris, I got to work with some fabulous people and I got to play.

The ritual of cleansing after a performance is very important. Some actors think it's only possible in the pub. The thing is, the body can't tell the difference between acting and reality. Whatever you've gone through on stage in the theatre is as real to your body as if you'd gone through it at home in your front room. You have to be very careful what you do with yourself after you've finished a performance. The trouble is it's late at night so the swimming pool and the sauna are probably closed, and you can't get a massage, so what do you do? Go and eat or drink; not a good idea late at night. It can be hard coming down after a performance – very hard. It's easy to have a dark night of the soul after a performance, and on a daily basis. It's when the drinking to oblivion often starts. I don't drink – I never have. If I'm in the UK I usually phone America because they're still up. In the past I've gone roller skating and dancing – lots of dancing. You don't want to talk, chances are you don't really want to think, you just want to come down. Sometimes I spend an inordinate amount of time in the ritual of taking off my make-up.

Beyond the Fourth Wall

I love theatre when it's alive – when I can feel a synergy between the actors and the audience. Pantomime is perfect for that. When Jude, my grandson, was six years old I played the Wicked Queen in *Snow White*. I wanted him to be able to see me in something he'd enjoy. It was the first time I'd done pantomime and I loved it. Unfortunately we forgot to explain the rules to Jude and he got really upset when everyone booed me. The first time it happened he stood up and shouted 'No!' After the show I explained that booing for baddies was their clapping. When he came to see the show again he was the most enthusiastic boo-er in the audience. He's going to look after his 'Glamma', that boy. He's never forgotten my Wicked Witch. I asked him what he thought after he came to see me play Maria Callas in *Master Class*. 'Hmmm,' he pondered, 'I think that was better than *Snow White*.' My Maria Callas did look a bit like a wicked queen.

Panto is hard graft, two shows a day, but it's a lot of fun. You're free to acknowledge the audience and play with them. A baby starts crying: 'Bring it here and I'll wring its neck.' You can come forwards and talk to your audience. Restoration comedy's like that, too. There's no imaginary fourth wall that you pretend the audience aren't behind.

If you're doing a Harold Pinter play, the audience isn't there. They have to exist for laughs and timing, but beyond that they're not there. They're not part of your experience on stage. You're just talking to other characters in a living room; there's nobody watching you.

Harold Pinter's meant to be quite highbrow so there's no playing allowed, but the naughtiest actors always find a way. In 1970 I did two Pinters in the West End, at The Duchess Theatre: *The Basement* and *The Tea Party*, both with Donald Pleasance and Barry Foster. Donald was always trying to make me laugh on stage. His character wore glasses and he played one of our scenes with his back to the audience. On one occasion, as the lights came up on stage, there were two grapes where Donald's eyes should have been. I tried to get him back but it was very hard – he was utterly concentrated. Then, during one of our performances when I was doing a staged leap, the crutch in my trousers ripped. Donald was shaking with laughter.

In the Sixties everybody had to take their clothes off at some point or other, even for Harold Pinter. There was a low-lit scene in which I had to undress and get into bed with Barry Foster. Then the set revolved and the next scene was me building a sandcastle in a bikini. While we were in the bed, looking like we were doing other things, Barry was helping me on with my bikini – only one night the bikini wasn't in the bed. I had to do a quick change in the wings, get back onto the revolving bed and straight onto the beach, lights up. I remember sitting on that beach building a sandcastle wondering whether my bikini was on straight. Without the fourth wall I could have played that completely differently.

When Ken Cranham's wig fell off during a performance of *The London Cuckolds*, I started laughing. It took away any discomfort or embarrassment the audience might have felt and they started laughing, too. That made Ken behave very badly. He started putting his wig back on upside-down and back-to-front until we were all in hysterics.

When I did *The Rover* with Jeremy Irons for the Royal Shakespeare Company in 1988, we had a similar moment. Jeremy did something that made me giggle. I can't remember what: a naughty wink, or a funny look or something. I told him to stop and the audience started laughing. Once they started, I couldn't stop. I was laughing so much I had to go and wipe my eyes on the curtains upstage. The audience adored seeing a film star and a television star enjoying being on stage together, and really cracking up. They felt that they were a part of something completely original, and they were.

With Rupert Everett in The Vortex

If you laugh and the audience sees what you're laughing at, your laughter will make them laugh, then their laughter will make you laugh even more; you can go on forever. It is great fun, but you've got to be very careful because you have to be able to pull the play back. It's *real* laughter, and it's a *real* moment. One moment the audience is just watching a play, then suddenly they're a part of the play, and everyone's wide awake.

Like Pinter, Noel Coward's plays happen behind the fourth wall. In 1991 I played Rupert Everett's mother Florence in Coward's *The Vortex* at the Ahmanson Theatre in Los Angeles.

After the production finished I took a trip to Sedona, Arizona. I wanted to spend some time in a terrestrial vortex. Sedona is known as a sacred site and also as the location of vortices of spiritual energy. It's set in quite an unusual and stunning red rocky landscape, in the highland of the Arizona desert. The red sandstone is totally unique to that area. One morning while I was meditating, sitting on one of the red rocks, the sun suddenly disappeared and I felt cold flecks on my skin. I opened my eyes. It was snowing, but only on the rock that my friend and I were sitting on. After a minute or two it stopped as suddenly as it had started. Then the sun came back out again.

Paid to Play

All through my life I've been tantalized with reminders of what happened on that rooftop at RADA. Very occasionally, when I'm on stage acting there is a perfect moment. If you stop and think, 'This is a good moment,' you'll dry up on the next. You can only acknowledge it after it's happened. There's an experience of energy and communication; something happens. It's about the synergy between the actors and the audience in the theatre.

RADA prepared me in so many ways for my career as an actress, including the experience on the rooftop. At the time it was another amazing new experience in a life that had been fuelled by new experiences. I put it in my medieval suede bag and it's always been there, casting a glow over my life.

Theatre is its own kind of magic. Hamri, a wise Moroccan expert on magic, told my anthropologist boyfriend Bernie:

> In the early human times there was magic everywhere, then over the millennia as mankind became civilized, magic declined and became ritual. Now in the modern world all that is left of true ritual is the theatre.

There's nothing fantastical about make-believe; fantastic, yes – because believing is three-quarters of the way to achieving. I don't have fantasies, I just make plans. I think of something fantastical and then I plan how I can make it happen. Everything begins as an idea, as a thought that bubbles up from the imagination. And being able to play, allowing yourself to play, exercises the imagination. The creative self is the God-self, born from the imagination. To create is to conjure an idea into existence; it's magic. Being a creator is not playing at being God; it really is drawing on that God-self we all carry within.

I'm exceptionally lucky – I'm paid to play.

When I was in *The Colbys* I remember Charlton Heston and me injecting magic into some very dull scenes. Never mind the fact that the peripherals of the show were all about gloss, we still cared that its content should have a spark of magic. That great star Charlton Heston was a grafter, and he had real integrity. I'd go up to him, and he'd say, 'Oh dear, I see the fingers are going,' because my fingers wiggle around when I've got ideas. And I'd say, 'Chuck, I've got this idea, because this looks rather bland the way it's been written,' and he always listened. We'd add subtext and superimpose meaning onto dull scenes, for the fun of it and because it made it a richer experience to do and to watch. As a rule, technicians – the chippies and sparks – don't bother to hang around the set during filming. They do their job, and then clear off. But when Chuck and I had a scene and the First Director called, 'Quiet on the set, we're ready for a run-through,' we'd gather an audience. They knew they'd get to see a little bit of theatre because we cared enough to want to create some magic.

It's a very interesting thing not to kowtow to an audience, but to woo them without being a whore; to gather them up. It's an art. It's usually about the cast working together, unless you're the main focal point on stage. When I toured *Master Class* in 2010–2011, I had sole responsibility for gathering the audience and taking them with me. The play's set inside the Juilliard School of Music. It's based around a master class being given by the great diva Maria Callas. For two hours, Maria talks to the audience as if they are Juilliard students. It was an extraordinary experience. The way I would woo them, the way I would gather them was different in each town. In Cheltenham, where everyone seemed to me to be so fragile and insecure, I had to be rather gentle and encouraging, whereas in Brighton the audience just adored Maria flagellating them!

My preparation before going on stage is sacred, and silent. Some people natter; I don't. I absolutely have to zone in. Immediately before going on I rub my hands together until I feel the energy all around myself, and then excitement. Then I just say, 'Let go, let God.' It's a ritual I've always done. It's all about me getting out of my own way; I get out of my way to let the higher power come in and guide me. I let go and let God.

Once on stage you have to be truly in the moment, following each one as it comes to pass. There's no living in the moment quite like there is on stage, apart from, perhaps, childbirth. If you're thinking ahead, you're mucking up. If you're doing a post-mortem about what went slightly icky a moment ago, you're mucking up. It's like skiing slalom – like downhill racing. You can't think 'I've just flicked that post'; you have to think, 'I've got to do this one and this one and this one.' With 'let go and let God', you are released to be in each and every moment of the performance, conscious and awake to its unique magic. If I didn't do this I'd be nervous, ego-ridden, fixated on wanting to do well, and fearful.

You can apply it to any situation that demands some kind of performance. If you're going for an interview, or to an important meeting, it's the only way to be. As long as you've done your best to prepare. After all, you've got to do the work – this isn't about expecting God to do it for you. If you've done your preparation, take off your mental pinny, wash your hands and say, 'Let go, let God.' Just be in the moment. Only put in the energy that each moment requires. Don't try too hard. Trying too hard is trying too hard. Trying too little is too little. Just be there. If you've done the work, just being there is enough.

Charlton Heston once said to me, 'We've got the best job in the world, but don't tell anyone. They'll all want to do it.' And I can remember Kenneth Cranham breathlessly exclaiming, as we came off stage during a performance of *The London Cuckolds*: 'Oh Steph, this is better than sex!' It's true; it can be a lot of fun – as well as hard work. And it's not just actors who have licence to play.

Chapter Four

Sixties Chic

I remember talking with a friend about whether she should buy a silver fox fur coat or do an acid trip with R D Laing. It was 1967 and we were at the epicentre of a movement that was sweeping the Western world. For a minute or six, love was there on the streets. It was tangible, it was vibrant and I was living in the front seat of a radical social experiment we were creating from one moment to the next. The whole of youth seemed to be involved in an expansion of consciousness. Our mentors and guides were magicians and wondrous folk.

R D Laing typified the time. A psychiatrist and psychotherapist, his approach to mental disorders drew as much on philosophy and real-life experience as it did on medical theory. Rather than individual people being mad, he thought it was society, and the institutions that control our lives, that were insane. In harmony with a spirit of the time, his approach was based on compassion and humane understanding. Though he was totally against the use of anti-psychotic drugs in the treatment of mental illness, he thought that mind-expanding drugs – like LSD and mescaline – had the potential to unlock the unlimited reservoir of our imaginations and give us insight into the wonders and mysteries of the universe. He was also an advocate of communal living. At Kingsley Hall, in East London, patients and therapists lived together; an experimental alternative, challenging what Laing thought was the inhuman system to which people with mental illnesses were usually subjected.

We were pushing against the world of our parents in order to gain momentum and move forwards. We wanted to do things our way – to smash the mental manacles that we felt had limited our parents' lives. We were fearlessly forging our way towards a brave new world. There were a lot of us, we were the post-war babies, and we were well educated. We could study whatever we wanted and get a grant for anything. You'd ask a friend what they were studying and they'd tell you Egyptology at Balliol or Theoretical Physics at Imperial. We wanted to learn. We wanted to know. We were changing the world.

The mores and hypocritical suburban attitudes that had underpinned our parents' lives were being challenged. We were bored by that suburban outlook. We wanted more. We wanted better. But we weren't prepared to have more war. The anti-Vietnam movement was huge. My American friends at RADA were either saying they were gay, attempting to get ulcers by eating toothpaste or going to Canada to avoid the draft. We all knew that Vietnam was a useless war and that the West had no right to be there. We were agents of love and we were absolute – and, mirroring the lack of compassion shown to returning GIs in the US, not particularly respectful of people who had fought in the Second World War.

The Commune

Soon after my rooftop experience I saw a note on the RADA noticeboard:

ACTRESS WANTED IN COMMUNE...
PHONE THIS NUMBER...

I did, and became one of eight people living together in a planned and conscious model of communal living. Unlike our parents, we weren't interested in getting married and settling into a predetermined order. People like R D Laing were saying that the nuclear family was a source of neurosis and dysfunction. We wanted to explore alternatives to the norm; different kinds of 'family'.

True communal living is about a lot more than simply sharing a house with other people. It takes work and effort. It demands structure, principles and rules. We wanted to be able to live in a family in which people didn't take each other for granted or disrespect one another. Learning not to be selfish, to be able to listen to others and share, took thought and practice. As members of a commune we had to be ready to put in the time to make it work. We were.

It wasn't that easy. If you're hung up about what you think is yours, and only yours, it's going to be a challenge. It was also about sharing your skills and labour and contributing to household maintenance; the mundane and routine and the fun and interesting. I learned so much from the people I was living with.

Our commune consisted of a sculptor and a silk-screen printing artist, both students at the Royal Academy of Arts, three architects studying at the Royal Institute of Architecture, Annie, who worked in publishing, and Judy, who partnered up with one of the architects and gave us Yossarian Yggdrasil, a gorgeous baby boy known as Yggy. There was also a cat, a hamster, and me.

Even the make-up of the commune's members was consciously worked out in order to try to create a balance of personalities and professions. Sharing our skills and professional expertise, debating philosophy and ideology, we created a rich and rewarding habitat in which to live and grow.

Communal living is a mini-society. If it's going to work, there's no room for ego. Unlike the hierarchical model of the family, with dad – or mum – at the top, followed by the older siblings and on down, the commune's field is level: no one's boss. Everything was done by consensus. You needed to make lots of compromises. Everything we did was discussed at length. We'd have long philosophical debates about the domestic rules of the house. Should we wash up before or after we'd eaten? If you were going to turn on the oven to bake a potato, should you let everyone else know so they'd have the chance to cook something as well, so the commune could save on fuel bills?

Middle-class children developing a new set of life values, we were making up the rules as we went along. We had a large noticeboard, which we called The Interpolation Board, where we jotted down anything we had bought. When we came to do the tally, if we thought one person wasn't as well off as another we'd 'interpolate' so they didn't have to pay as much as others who were better off. We had an extraordinary sense of commune. We had detailed conversations. If I break this Minton china teacup, can I replace it with another vessel that holds liquid? What are we dealing with? Is it a vessel for holding liquid or is it the aesthetic of bone china? Our conclusion was that beauty was where *you* saw it, and manufactured beauty wasn't of that much interest – a vessel was just a vessel. So, if you broke someone's Minton cup it could be replaced with a mug from Woolworths.

We were far from unique – back then there were a lot of people living in the same way; some similar to the way we were doing it and some more experimentally, like R D Laing's community at Kingsley Hall. We were learning how to live with others – and be laid back. You'd hope people would try to use their own toothbrush, but if someone used your toothpaste, it wasn't important. What was important was that we were all just people trying to survive and share.

We shared all the influences of that era. Dylan, the Mothers of Invention, The Beatles – we actually had a party the day *Sgt. Pepper's* was released. Our reading list included Gurdjieff, Castaneda, the I Ching, the underground newspaper *International Times*, *Rolling Stone* magazine and, of course, *Private Eye*. We laughed a lot, we learned a lot, and had a really good time.

Gradually, though, I found myself putting my individual needs above the communal needs and it was time to move on. My career had started and I needed a different way of living. I wasn't a student any more. I had to go to bed at 9 p.m. if I was going to get up at 5 a.m. to be on a film set. For a lot of people at that time, living was a career. I was no longer prepared to see a drinking vessel simply as a drinking vessel. I wanted to have nice things from Heals that wouldn't be replaced from Woolworths if they got broken. I was developing taste as well as philosophy.

Mescaline

In the end my girlfriend decided on R D Laing, not the fox fur coat. Drugs like LSD and mescaline were not taken recreationally. People approached them with a sense of purity and purpose. They were treated with respect, and the potential consequences of what might happen if they weren't used responsibly were not taken lightly. We took it for granted that your mind, your soul and your spirit could be accessed through very carefully monitored psychedelic trips. If you were deciding to take a trip, it was done responsibly. You'd find a safe, beautiful place; you'd get your toys out, paints, good food, and the right people. LSD and mescaline were used to experience a higher level of consciousness, and were completely in line with anyone who was spiritually seeking. Taking these drugs responsibly involved having a friend with you who hadn't taken anything to act as a guide, facilitating you to use the trip most effectively.

I took mescaline once and had an extraordinarily powerful experience. I encountered a previous incarnation in a mirror. He was a South American Indian. It was completely riveting. Well, I thought it was; I stayed in front of that mirror for about an hour. Then I went outside into a field and saw my own funeral pyre. At first I was terrified, but then I gently started kicking at my skeleton and it turned to dust. I experienced the phrase 'ashes to ashes and dust to dust' as a totally lucid and vivid reality. I experienced the truth that matter is never destroyed – merely changed.

I came back from the experience with the knowledge that death is inevitable and nothing to be afraid of; that it's part of a circle and a cycle – the circle of life and the cycle of death and rebirth.

Transcendental Meditation

London in the 1960s – there were so many things happening. You couldn't help but get caught up. My first introduction to meditation came through Guru Maharishi Mahesh Yogi's technique of Transcendental Meditation. He got a huge profile in the UK after The Beatles adopted him as their guru. We were all investigating, searching, exploring. I went along, too, in my Afghan coat, with a flower and an offering of some money and was given a word to chant.

It was very *Barefoot in the Park* – delightful but not particularly deep. We all sat there, breathing and meditating. It didn't feel like an internal experience but was wonderful fun. I'm glad I did it. I didn't have to use it again until many years later when I had to lie still in a hospital room for three weeks with my second daughter Chloe inside me, to prevent her from being born prematurely after my waters broke too soon.

At any time a situation can arise and you pull out what's already inside you. Suddenly it comes to the fore. During the 1960s I was having a good time. I wasn't doing things for my survival. I was playing and also hoping for more experiences that come out of nowhere – like Versailles and the RADA rooftop.

I was experimenting for experimentation's sake and there were so many opportunities to do just that.

Synergy and Synchronicity

I was eager and hungry to learn. At a lecture given by Buckminster Fuller, the American engineer, theorist and futurist, I was completely blown away. It was the first time I'd come across the

61

concepts 'synergy' and 'synchronicity'.

He gave a scientific explanation of synergy. It went something like this: if you know the prehensile strength of this metal and you know the prehensile strength of that metal, you'd imagine you understood the strength of these two metals joined together. But, in fact, these two metals joined together have an exponentially greater strength; so, too, when human beings join together. This is synergy – unexpected but scientifically true.

We are meant to join together. We have the potential to do so much more when joined than we ever could achieve alone. Team effort, the power of the group, the strength of the commune, a congregation of believers or the experience of good theatre are all synergetic experiences.

The term 'synchronicity' was first coined by Carl Jung – a Swiss psychiatrist and spiritual seeker. He used it to refer to the way seemingly unrelated and – on the surface – disconnected events come together in a deeply meaningful way: always with a message and sometimes with profound implications. Deepak Chopra calls it 'synchrodestiny'. These events are like miracles; reminding us that *all* things are connected.

Synchronicity is like having the stage curtains pulled back to reveal a perfect scene that had been there all the time – you just couldn't see it. It's like having the lights go up on a pattern that's somehow shaping your life. It's definitely in the realm of fractals – those incredible self-replicating geometric shapes that were first created by mathematicians, then discovered to exist everywhere in Nature.

Sometimes things appear to come together in a moment; sometimes over a period of hours, weeks, months or even years.

Our lives join up; just like a good haircut.

The way I landed in *The London Cuckolds* at The Royal Court back in 1979 is a good example of how things often join up in unexpected ways.

I'd been in *The Singular Life of Albert Nobbs* with Susannah York at the New End Theatre, Hampstead. It was directed by Simone Benmussa, a tiny French visionary who used lighting and music in the production in a way I'd never experienced before. I wanted to introduce Simone to Stuart Burge, who was The Royal Court's artistic director. Stuart had directed me in Ibsen's *The Doll's House* at the Nottingham Playhouse a few years earlier.

While we were having tea, Stuart asked me what I was doing the next day. I told him I didn't know. Then he asked me what I was doing for the next couple of months. I told him that I wasn't sure. I was entering a very difficult and dark period in my life. The way I replied characterized the uncertainty of that time. Stuart gave me a script that he had with him and told me to read it – it was *The London Cuckolds*. He called me later and said he was casting. He told me to come along. It just came out of the blue; I wasn't looking to be cast, I was just looking to make the introduction. I wasn't thinking of acting; I just wanted to bring together two people I thought would have synergy.

I find the way things work best is not to connive and contrive but to try to maintain a spirit of generosity; to be open to possibility and, rather than thinking 'I want,' to think 'I'm ready and I'm willing.'

In 1996, when we were on Broadway in Sir Peter Hall's production of Oscar Wilde's *An Ideal Husband*, Nicky Henson, who was playing Lord Goring, and I shared an apartment. One morning I went out to get a latte. When I got back Nicky was doing the washing up, whistling happily. He looked at me. 'Did you go out like that?' he asked. 'Yes,' I replied, looking down at my Ugg boots and fur coat over my nightdress. 'You're a slut,' he said, and merrily carried on washing up. 'And you're squeaky,' I muttered. We looked at each other and burst out laughing. That's what we've called each other ever since. The following year Peter took Slut and Squeaky to Australia when he was asked to do the play in Sydney, Melbourne and Brisbane. While there we became good friends with John McCallum and Googie Withers. Married since 1948, they lived in Australia. Both were part of the cast for the play's tour there.

In 2000 John and Googie came to Bristol to do a play called *A Busy Day* written by the 18th-century novelist, playwright and diarist, Fanny Burney. I went to see them on the opening night. My daughter Phoebe was living in Bristol and her son Jude had just been born, so it was all perfect. But Googie was ill and her understudy was on. John told me he thought the play was going to transfer to the West End. People often say that about plays in the provinces, and it usually doesn't happen. Then he asked me if I'd play Googie's part if it went to the West End. I told him I'd be delighted, not for a minute thinking it would transfer. I saw the play, didn't think any more about it, and got on with being Granny.

The run took its course, then the day before the play was being taken off they suddenly got a West End contract. We were opening in ten days and I had to learn the most difficult script you could imagine. It wasn't easy like Shakespeare, where you've got your metrical feet and your iambic pentameter and you know what you're meant to be doing. This was impossible, it was Regency English: it was a skating rink. And I was taking over from an 84 year old. I was taking over from Googie – a wonderful, big, elderly woman. I suddenly had to fabricate a character out of nowhere. Working alongside the designer Rory Murchison, we came up with all these concepts and fun ideas about how I'd do it and what should happen. That's when I met Jonathan Church, the play's director.

Immediately after doing *A Busy Day*, Jonathan took over as artistic director of the Birmingham Repertory Theatre. One of the first plays he did there was Timothy Findley's *Elizabeth Rex*. He asked me to play Elizabeth I. He'd seen the way I'd jumped into *A Busy Day* with more than two solid feet, playing an outrageous, elderly dowager duchess. In *Elizabeth Rex* I had to play the 62-year-old Queen Elizabeth I – older than I was at the time, but that wasn't a problem. It was a joy.

One day in 2009, my friend Ronnie Roberts, who I'd met doing *Tenko*, told me she'd had a dream the night before in which I was channelling Maria Callas. Years earlier the film director Franco Zeffirelli had told me I was the spitting image of her. He was so shocked he actually fell back in the chair he was sitting on: 'You *are* Maria Callas,' he told me – as if I were her ghost. At the time Ronnie was working with Jonathan Church. She told him about her dream, too.

In 2010 my dear friend Christopher Cazenove died suddenly. It took Christopher dying to make me think, 'If not now, when?' I got on the phone and called Jonathan, asking him if he remembered Ronnie telling him about her dream. I told him Ronnie had told me, too. He said we should meet and talk about it.

Later that year I *was* playing Maria Callas, on stage in *Master Class*.

A Busy Day, *Elizabeth Rex* and *Master Class* are three of the strongest pieces of theatre I've done; none of them because I was lucky enough to know the head of casting at 20th Century Fox, or anything like that. All of them came out of loving friendships and the way separate paths crossed at specific points: opening the curtains for the miracle of synchronicity.

You'd be absolutely spot-on if you said, 'What's so unusual? That's the way life is.' You'd be right. It's not unusual. Life is a miracle. Our existence *is* magic.

Ronnie was right, too. I *did* channel Maria. When I was doing the show in Edinburgh – on the same stage where she had performed – in the middle of a monologue, she came and had a word in my ear. Crazy woman!

Being Greedy

Soon after I left RADA in 1967 I worked at the Oxford Playhouse with the great director Frank Hauser.

One day I was late for rehearsals. I rushed into the theatre making my apologies.

'How late are you?' Frank asked me.

'Two minutes…' came my breathless reply.

'And how many people are in the room?'

'Thirty?' I answered.

'Well, in that case, I make it 60 minutes late, then.'

That was embarrassing. I was thoroughly ashamed. It was an invaluable lesson, though. Ever since, whether I'm on stage or set, I make it my business never to be late. I'd learned from professionals like Frank that having a thoroughly professional attitude is *the* foundation for success.

Another time he commented on how 'greedy' I was as an actor.

'I mean that as a compliment,' Frank reassured me, when I'd looked taken aback. 'You know that lovely young actress Judi Dench?' he asked. 'She's greedy, too.'

Personally, I prefer to call it 'enthusiastic'. If I commit to something, I commit totally. What's the point of doing otherwise?

Around the same time I was working with Frank I got a guest role in the television series *The Saint*.

The Saint was one of the most popular shows on television at the time and its lead actor, Roger Moore, was a household name. Waiting for our first scene together, I whispered to him: 'It's my birthday today!' Raising that famous eyebrow he responded:

'You don't say that every time you work, do you?'

'No, seriously – I'm 21 today,' I replied.

'It's your 21st birthday? Well, that's quite a thing.'

When we wrapped for the day, Roger presented me with a card. He'd drawn it himself. The set was closed down, a cake was brought in and we drank champagne.

The Last Waltz

Those times were joyous, alive, mind-opening and, for a short patch of time, the love was there on the streets. I am so grateful I was there to experience it. I wasn't at the Stones' free concert in Hyde Park when they released hundreds of butterflies to honour

Brian Jones. At the time I was co-starring with Ava Gardner and Ian McShane in *Tam Lin* in Scotland.

But I did get to the Isle of Wight to see Bob Dylan, and I found myself standing three feet away from Jimi Hendrix at the fundraising concert *The 14 Hour Technicolour Dream* at Alexandra Palace. It was a wonderful time to be young.

What happened to the hippie ideal? By the early 1970s too many people were dying from bad drugs. In the US too many people from unhappy backgrounds in the Midwest were moving to the West Coast. There were too many false gurus. The purity had gone. It had become dysfunctional.

I moved out of the commune just as the sun was going down.

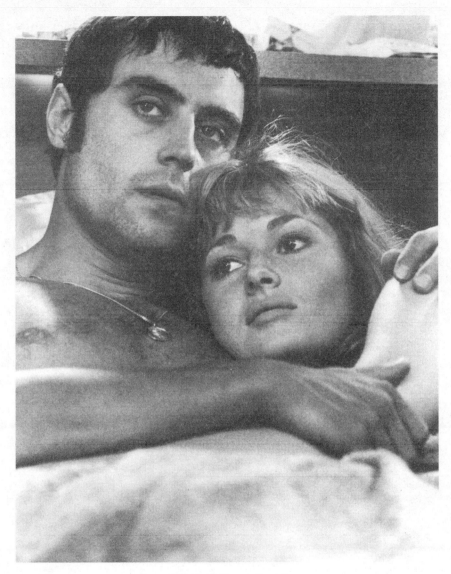

With Ian McShane in Tam Lin

Chapter Five

When Kids Have Kids

Phoebe

We'd arrived at the hospital and my contractions were happening every three minutes. I'd brought a nightie, a Mars bar and my sewing kit. I didn't really think this was *it* – I still had three weeks to go. Suddenly there I was, being hideously shaved by the roughest nurse, who could have worked for the Gestapo. I dragged my husband John into a bathroom, locked the door and got into the bath. 'Give me a cigarette,' I demanded. 'This is ghastly.' I had to regroup, to stop the hospital taking over. They seemed to think they owned me, and I wasn't going to let *that* happen. This was *our* child and *my* birth experience. John went rushing off and bought tons of freesias. I was deep-breathing to the beautiful smell of flowers. It was completely magical. It was a perfect birth.

The next day was God-filled. A nurse found me weeping and asked if I was all right. 'Oh, yes,' I said. 'I'm more all right than I could ever imagine being.' God was golden in my heart and in my soul. I was weeping with gratitude for my beautiful child. Phoebe was *so* perfect. Everybody else's baby was so ugly. I felt sorry for them. I didn't know that's how all new mothers feel.

Phoebe had been born on 29th December. On New Year's Eve I was sitting with some other mums on our rubber rings. We were at that bad time – third day in – when the glory's over and reality's kicking in and you're very sore and your milk's coming in and it really isn't a good feeling. John, his brother and my young nephew bribed their way with champagne to the fifth floor of the hospital. They'd brought a crate of the stuff. 'Hold on... you can't... Oh, Happy New Year!' And in they came to this diverse group of mums and babies, and got us all completely merry. We had thought no one was going to be bringing in the New Year with us. Everybody else's husband was off at this party or that. We had a great time, and the next day all our babies slept for ages.

We brought in 1975 very well. Anyone capable of instigating such fun is bound to be trouble.

That was John.

He and I had been a sparkling couple. We'd raced fast. We had a Jaguar XK150. He'd played Mercutio in Franco Zeffirelli's multiple-Oscar-nominated film *Romeo and Juliet*. I'd already starred in films with Marlon Brando and Ava Gardner. We both loved to play. He had his flying machine and I had my doll's house. We played like kids. Regardless of the time of day or night, we went with the game of the moment. We'd been to A-list parties but decided we didn't like that life, and had taken our vows, made a home and started a family.

John

I first met John McEnery when I was 17. We were both working at the Liverpool Everyman Theatre. He was 21 and one of their leading actors. Once, while I was at The Everyman, John had taken me out for a bowl of soup at the local greasy spoon. I'd found myself rather stuck for things to say. He was this leading man, on the cusp of great things – soon after he'd be invited to join the National Theatre. One weekend we'd all gone to the Lake District for a break. John arrived with a girl from London. She had a Vidal Sassoon haircut and a kitten; very sophisticated – very Chelsea. I was just a wardrobe assistant playing juvenile leads.

It was seven years later when I got a part in Shakespeare's *The Tempest* at The Nottingham Playhouse that I met John properly again. He was playing Ariel. Playing a spirit totally suited his mercurial nature. My friend Marsha Hunt used to call him 'John McMercury'.

When *The Tempest* finished its run, John and I were cast to play opposite each other in The Playhouse's next production: Harold Pinter's *The Homecoming*.

Rife with sexual tension, *The Homecoming* is more about what's not said between its characters than what's said. The atmosphere on stage was electric between us. John and I took that off stage as well. It was intense. We were on fire. We became inevitable. We were soon living together.

John was vibrant, charismatic; full of life and brimming with energy. He was a very striking man to look at: blond hair, piercing blue eyes, a tall and slender frame. Around John you always had the sense that something quite unexpected might happen. We danced on an electrifying high wire.

John McEnery

And then there was his talent. I defy any woman not to fall for a man who exudes it. In terms of fame and fortune, John was devoid of ambition. In terms of his craft, he shone with a passion. Every performance was packed with everything he had to give, no matter how big or small the role. To watch him on stage was to watch a master at his craft.

And more – he was unpredictable. That was exciting. He was the first person I'd met who could react as fast as I could. The only trouble was, there was no thought between the idea and the action.

There was also a shadow of misery cloaking him, with an underlying difficultness I found both intriguing and challenging. Foolish woman that I was, I thought I could save him.

I loved this man – this totally irresponsible, incorrigible man.

We went to Tunisia. It felt like a honeymoon. John asked me to marry him and I said 'yes.'

Back in London we arranged our wedding for three days later. My sisters Didi and Jenny and my brother Richard were living abroad and couldn't arrange to be back in England in time. My father said he was playing golf and couldn't get out of it. It didn't matter. Mummy came and wore a big hat. All we wanted was to get married.

The day before the wedding, while we were shopping for strawberries and champagne for the reception, John asked me what I planned to wear. I hadn't given it any thought. He went missing for the rest of afternoon, returning three hours later with a dress and a pair of shoes.

I'd never seen a dress quite so beautiful and extraordinary. It was a very simple tunic of two layers of white cotton. If you pulled the top layer up, it could be worn as a veil. It was unique and of its time, and very me. I was amazed that my husband-to-be could get it so right at a moment's notice. I couldn't have chosen a more perfect outfit. He wore one of my white silk shirts.

That was John.

Our friend Andrew McAlpine, an incredibly gifted art director, made me a bouquet of magnolia blossoms, and my two King Charles Cavalier Spaniels stood in as bridesmaids. My first dog, Amoreena, had been a gift from Michael Winner and Marlon Brando when we'd finished *The Nightcomers*. When she had puppies I kept one and called her Minnie. On the day of my wedding, with their leads and collars adorned with flowers, Amoreena and Minnie scratched their way through the service.

During the reception the reality of what we had committed to hit me. This was for real, it wasn't a game. It was for life. To me, that was really important.

John's wedding ring accidentally went down the drain the day after we were married. 'I never *did* like wearing rings,' was all he could say.

That was John.

Soon after we were married I became pregnant. I was delighted. The thought of motherhood and children hadn't crossed my mind before I'd fallen in love with John. When that happened, my values changed. Now all I wanted was a family. My career suddenly meant very little. Even so, I decided to change agents so I could be represented by the same one as John – thinking it best if one person was in charge of both our careers and working lives. So began a long, for-richer-or-poorer, for-better-or-worse, till-death-us-do-part relationship with the brilliant Maureen Vincent at United Agents. It's outlasted my other marriage by 30 years.

Wedding day – nice hat, Mummy!

I was just under three months pregnant when John and I were cast to play the roles of Hamlet and Ophelia in a production of *Hamlet* at the Edinburgh Festival. But my pregnancy ruled me out of playing the Prince's deranged, sickly and erstwhile love interest. It was decided I should play his other love interest, Gertrude – his mother.

At the beginning of the play Hamlet berates Gertrude for having married his uncle so soon after his father's death. During rehearsal, and in character, John pushed me and I fell. I had a miscarriage and spent three weeks in the Royal Infirmary. We both blamed ourselves for what had happened – vain, uncompromising actors, putting our art above all else. It was a painful lesson.

Months later we were in Scotland again, staying with friends. On the day of our return to London I asked them to take a picture of us standing in front of John's Jaguar.

'Why do you want a photo?' they asked.

'I just do,' I replied. I knew I could feel new life inside me. I was right. Phoebe was already waving.

Despite the Gestapo nurse but aided by John's flowers, the birth went as smoothly as I could have wished. When the baby was crowning, just beginning to come out, John was so excited he said, 'Look, it's coming!' and pushed my head down to see, and I nearly bumped heads with my baby – only John being John.

When he first held her, he looked at her face and said, 'Oh, it was you all the time.'

Our Nuclear Family

In 1969, with the fee I'd earned for my role in the film *Tam Lin*, I'd bought a flat in Hampstead. John had a Georgian sandstone on top of a hill in Nottingham. We trailed between the two – car packed with carrycot, pram and dogs. I slipped seamlessly into the role of being a mother. I adored my baby. Her tiny fingers, her big bright eyes, the expressions and noises she made. She brought me such joy. I cooked, I cleaned and I stitched and sewed; making her clothes, smocking her little dresses. It was the beginning of a new life for me. My career now felt secondary – somehow rather unfulfilling and dull. I only wanted to work if it didn't take me too far from Phoebe and the hours weren't too long. It was as if my eagerness and ambition had left; now channelled as love for my baby. I still cared for my craft, but babies and family life had become more important.

And God's golden light continued to glow for me – bringing me work I could do on *my* terms. A couple of months after Phoebe's birth I was in Pete Walker's *The Confessional* with Norman Eshley and Susan Penhaligon – or Susie Pen*hooligan*, as I call her. It was filmed in St John's Wood, just round the corner from the flat.

It was a really bad movie, but very convenient. I took Phoebe to work in her basket.

'How long are we going to be waiting for the lighting?' Pete would ask while we waited for the sparks. 'Come on, Stephanie's tits are filling up.' It was great; I was working and still attached to my bubba. Pete: 'Was that the kid mewling? (sigh) Let's go for another take.' Pete was lovely.

John came with me to the screening. He was totally silent throughout. When it was over, he turned to Pete. 'How much did that cost to produce?' he asked. What else could he say? It was unspeakably bad, and I wouldn't have missed doing it for the world.

I took to being a mother with ease, but for John, despite the fact that he was besotted with Phoebe, parenthood was a huge challenge. Ten days after she'd been born I left her with him while I popped to the shops. 'She's bathed, she's changed and she's asleep,' I told John as I reached for my coat. 'All you have to do is keep an eye on her.'

I got back 20 minutes later. Phoebe wasn't in her cot. 'John, where's Phoebe?' I asked, slightly bewildered.

'Ah…' he responded. My heart sank. Whenever John said 'Ah…' it was always a sign he'd done something… odd.

A trail of baby clothes – a cardigan, a babygro, a tiny hat – led to the bedroom. I followed them. Phoebe was hanging by her hands from the ladder to our platform bed. She was stark naked. Her face had turned puce.

I scooped her into my arms. 'Phoebe's stark naked and hanging from a ladder!' I yelled.

'Yes,' he said, following me into the room, quite unperturbed by my obvious shock and horror.

'I thought she needed her back stretched,' he explained. 'I read about it in the paper – it's that baby monkey theory. If you hang a baby from a ladder they *can* sustain their weight. Didn't you know?'

'But she's 10 days old!'

'I thought it'd be good for her. Anyway, she looked a little hot in all those cardigans – all wrapped up like that.'

'Hot, John? It's January.'

That was John.

He always did these things with the best of intentions, though.

A few months after our second daughter Chloe was born in 1977, I was working on Pirandello's *The Old and the Young* in Italy. She'd been quite a sickly baby since she'd been born and now she'd gone down with pneumonia. The Italian doctors had put her on a huge dose of antibiotics that weren't working. I was phoning specialists in Rome to see if she'd been prescribed the right medication. Meanwhile, she wasn't getting any better. Back home, John had gone missing and I didn't know how to reach him. It was a nightmare and I was getting more and more distraught. Following the advice of the doctors in Rome, I had Chloe wrapped up in a darkened room. Finally John turned up. I didn't know where he'd been, but suddenly he arrived in Italy. He walked in,

My handsome father

Happy to be here — with Mummy

Family holiday in Devon.
Left to right: Richard, me, Mummy, Daddy, Didi

At age three

At age eight and hardly Hollywood material

Best ear forward

My 21st birthday. Left to right: Richard, Didi, me, Jenny, Mummy, Daddy

With Marlon Brando in The Nightcomers

With John in The Homecoming

With Robert Powell, Peter Stringfellow half in, half out

With Phoebe on Rupert – Dartmoor

Pammy and me – Dartmoor

At This Is Your Life in Los Angeles. Left to right: Mummy, Me, Didi, Jenny

Chloe and Phoebe in their pink dresses

Comedian Chloe with missing teeth

With Phoebe, Chloe and Emily the dog

Daughters' confirmations at Wells cathedral.
Left to right: Little Sue, Christina, Daddy, Chloe, Emily, me, Mummy, Phoebe

Family rollerblading, Venice, California

With Phoebe and Chloe (© Patrick Lichfield)

At charity dinner with Nolan Miller, wearing Nolan Miller

Brits on Broadway
Left to right: me, James Warwick, Lucy Flemming, Simon Williams, Nicky Henson, Ian Ogilvy

pulled open the shutters, tore open the windows, took Chloe out of her cot and took off every stitch of her clothing. He marched out of the room and the next thing I heard was a splash – he'd jumped into the swimming pool with her.

I'd been doing what the doctors in Rome had told me. John just walked in and thought, 'This is ridiculous.' She got better quite quickly after that.

John did things his way.

I got home from work one afternoon and couldn't find the dogs. It was pouring with rain. I asked, 'Where are the dogs, John?' Then I heard a whimpering sound, which I followed out into the garden. I found them. There they were, forlorn and rain-drenched, on the flat roof of the kitchen. John said they'd been getting under his feet.

Children came as a massive shock. Suddenly I was at the beck and call of a tiny, needy pink thing. Nature gives mothers instincts; maybe the hormones that are released into the body during pregnancy prepare you for motherhood. I fell into motherhood with enormous joy. Men are less fortunate. John had a moment of elation and then, suddenly, life was all about the pram and the paraphernalia of babyhood.

In our house in Nottingham we'd had three rooms laid out with Scalextric. It was very elaborate, with bends, bridges, chicanes, pit stops, trees and little people waving us on. I was a John Player Special – very sleek and black – and John was a red Ferrari. When Phoebe was born, I sold half of the track. I don't think John ever forgave me. We had to get other toys and they weren't our toys any more; they were for a baby. He had to get rid of the XK150. It was a hopeless car for a baby and two dogs.

John's a one-off wonder, but a good and sensible husband? No. He's a true artist – completely selfish. That's what true artists are. They have to serve their art. They can't help it. Any good bit of work I did, I was a less good parent.

I think if you have a baby you should make a contract with your partner which says, 'For the first five years of this child's life we just get on with it. We'll look after our child and won't even discuss whether we love each other, and we won't break up.' The truth is, if you break off a relationship you'll come across the same problem in your next one because, guess what, you take yourself with you. We'd had the heady 1960s but we hadn't got to the age of self-help books, let alone good therapy. Back then we'd only got as far as discussing Freud or Jung.

When you're tending to and loving your baby for at least 15 hours of the day, it's very hard to want to be tending to your husband, too. Maybe he should be tending to the two of you. Joseph is standing behind Mary, looking after Mary, who's looking after Jesus. The man is not meant to be in competition with the baby. You only have a few. Let's do the baby now.

Make sure your man wants to have a child, because otherwise he may not be able to be as responsible as you'd like him to be. Do we listen to what our men say? They usually tell us the truth, in actions if not words. Or do we decide on a man based on what we think we need? I've got friends with biological clocks ticking who have made unsuitable choices and then been amazed when their partners haven't behaved properly. Their men told them the truth but they didn't want to hear it. Half the time, we don't listen to each other.

Everybody has to learn what they have to learn in his or her own way, but I think we have a huge number of questions to ask ourselves about the kind of parents we became. I'm talking about us freedom-seekers of the 1960s. We're a very selfish generation and we've bred an even more selfish one, and it's our fault. But then isn't everything that our kids do that's difficult our fault? It's only the good things they do that are them. I could write a book about that.

Rather than taking away our ability to play, children rewrite the way we can play. Like nothing else, apart from acting, they give us licence to play. Children have free access to the imagination. They're closer to the source, closer to the creative self – that is, the God-self. Half the time they're the ones playing while we're the ones sighing and tidying up. Have a good play with them, we can all tidy up later.

Chloe

Chloe was born in 1977. Her birth was very difficult. Two months before she was due, my membranes ruptured and I was losing amniotic fluid. I went to hospital immediately and was told labour would start within 24 hours, and that I had to stay there because I was no longer sterile and my baby was at risk of infection. I asked them at what stage of development my baby was. Her chances of survival didn't sound good. They put me in a small ward on strict bed-rest. I lay on the bed and breathed, feeling my baby's tiny body inside me. No longer with any fluid to act as a cushion, I could feel her skeleton – this still baby inside me was not moving. I just lay completely prone and breathed. I knew this baby had to 'cook' for longer. Guru Maharishi's Transcendental Meditation came into its own. Everyone had been given a mantra. I couldn't remember mine. I made one up. I concentrated on my breathing, and concentrated on the mantra. Slowly the amniotic fluid replaced itself. 'Baby... Live... Baby... Live...'

Meanwhile, back home, I'd left Phoebe with John. My parents had gone to stay to help with Phoebe, but they couldn't cope with John. They lasted a couple of days and then left. Phoebe got her head stuck in the cat flap and the fire brigade had to be called out. Then she managed to get her hands on a bottle of Calpol. She drank its contents and slept for 24 hours. I knew I had to get home.

I asked the doctor if my baby was viable. I was in hospital trying to save the life of one baby, while the welfare of my other one was at serious risk. It felt time for this baby to come out. I was induced. Chloe was born three weeks early. She'd been due on my birthday but came into the world an Aquarian. An hour after Chloe was born, as far as the hospital was concerned, I went missing. I didn't. I'd picked up this little newborn bundle and taken us both to a bathroom that had a bath you walked down into. I filled it with water and poured in salt and iodine, and sat in it. It was very uncomfortable. My little bundle was on the side of the bath at eye level. 'It's just you, me and your sister now, honey,' I told her.

It was hard for John to accept 'the full catastrophe' of a wife and two kids. He just wasn't up to it; it was down to me. I was determined to get out and get home as soon as possible. The love had left the household and I had to look after my babies. I was beginning a new life which I'd brought upon myself.

Chapter Six

Running on Empty

I remember watching a programme on TV back in 1977 called *Rock Follies*. I was sitting in my brown candlewick dressing gown. It had a zip down its front for baby's easy feeding access. It wasn't glamorous. I was staring at the television, thinking, 'I used to do that.' I never thought I'd be a human being again, let alone a vibrant one. I really thought I'd done myself in. Born too soon, Chloe was sick. She was finding it very difficult to latch on and feed. When she did she thew up – projectile vomiting. I had to take her back to the hospital. It was hard. It was frantically horrible.

My husband didn't love me any more. All communication was gone and I didn't know why. I didn't know that when someone feels guilty they can't talk to you. Six weeks after Phoebe was born in 1974, I'd been back making a movie. This time was very different. I couldn't sleep. Because Chloe wasn't feeding properly I had to wake her every two hours to try to get her to feed. In the morning I had to cope with a two-year-old bouncing off the walls.

I remember a moment of silence. 'Ahh, silence,' then, 'Silence?' I ran to the stairs. Phoebe had Chloe's head, and her friend Claire, another two-year-old, had her feet. They were swinging her, about to see if she'd bounce down the stairs.

After I'd put the children to bed at 6:30 p.m. the world used to close down around me. With no test card and music, just a blank screen. I couldn't even go out for a walk. Simply going down the garden to get the washing from the line, my ears would be constantly peeled, listening out for the babies. For a young woman – a young selfish woman, who's co-starred in movies, on stage and TV, and who's grown used to having her own money – to find herself suddenly alone and broke with two young babies and thinking she can't cope without her husband; it felt like I'd really mucked up my life.

John and I had decided to have a trial separation. He'd gone to Stratford-upon-Avon to work with the Royal Shakespeare Company. I didn't think I would be able to manage on my own without him. Phoebe was going through the terrible twos. I had to make a conscious decision to still allow some love for John. If I didn't I knew I wouldn't be able to love Phoebe and Chloe. I think you have to have love for the father or you won't have true love for your baby – you're trapped. It felt like a real decision I had to make. Now it hardly seems real – this old friend of mine, this silly old actor – it was another life. At the time, though, it was heart-breaking. I've always said John's a splendid actor but a ridiculous husband.

How could he leave? I was totally disbelieving. I kept thinking he'd come to his senses. How can you have a young wife and two babies and just leave them like that? I was convinced he'd come back, but he didn't. Truth is, I was running on empty before Chloe was born. I had no understanding of marriages not working. You made your vows, put on your ring and made it work. Nobody in my family got separated or divorced. I took my vows seriously, and now I felt my little tribe had been betrayed. I guess I should have had a clue when John lost his ring down the drain.

The problem with adultery is the conspiracy. Other people know what you don't. On the level of personal pride it's really hurtful, and the conspiracy leads to people avoiding you. My isolation became horrible. I couldn't understand why friends were staying away. I thought it was because I was toxic in my misery. I'm sure I was, but it was more than that. They had information that I didn't. When I did find out what had been going on, my world completely cracked apart.

I wish I hadn't been brought up with Walt Disney. I wish I hadn't had this expectation that "one day your prince will come" and, when he comes, that's it. It's so sadly unrealistic. The dishonesty of the conspiracy, the lying: when truth is withheld – it's crippling. Being unfaithful to the one you love is a disloyalty and it's not fair; it *is* a conspiracy. There was that attempt in the Sixties for free love, but we weren't up to it. We did a distortion. Partner-up if you want, but if you can't do it honestly, then don't do it.

Before John went to Stratford he was always going missing. One time I had a full plate of meat and roast potatoes, gravy, peas; the lot. John was on his way out of the door to go and see a man about a dog or whatever he was doing. I told him if he went the plate was going on the ceiling. He just looked at me and kept walking. I threw the plate so hard the peas embedded themselves in the plaster. They dried there and had to be painted over.

When Chloe was five months old John and I both got work in Sheffield – in plays at The Crucible Theatre. I was being directed by Peter James in Alan Ayckbourn's *Absurd Person Singular* and John was in Gogol's *The Government Inspector*. We shared a flat with Hildegarde Neil, Brian Blessed and their baby, and I had my two. It was above a rice and curry store. Strangely, it was the perfect way to get back into work. Phoebe started saying 'Mummy's working' in a Sheffield accent and John was John. One night we had a visit from the police. John had performed one of his very special tricks. He'd done it before and he's done it again since. It involves racing against flashing blue lights. When he was finally stopped and taken to the police station, he jumped on the station desk, telling them they couldn't arrest him because he was the government inspector. He was completely drunk. Sheffield had its moments of fun but Sheffield was difficult.

Back in London I was on my own again with the girls. I'd walk up and down Kilburn High Road looking for the cheapest tomatoes. 'Eggy-in-the-Nest' became our favourite meal. I did what work I could, but money was tight. An egg on spinach is a very cost-effective *and* nutritious dish.

Once, I had a matinee performance and the babysitter was late. I had to leave. I left a note outside for the babysitter, put Chloe in her basket, and took her and Phoebe over the road to the convent opposite our house. I knocked on its imposing front door. Two hairy nuns answered. Phoebe looked up at them, doe eyed, while they peered down on the slumbering Chloe – wrapped in swaddling clothes, lying in a basket. Their faces softened. I explained my predicament and they took the girls in. I whispered a word of thanks to Mary as I passed her statue in the garden.

I don't think they suffered from the experience; and they were given their first chocolate. Phoebe took to using a chair to reach the door handle to open the front door. She'd sneak across the road where she'd pick flowers from the convent's garden, knock on the door and exchange them for sweets with the nuns.

We were living in a huge house in West Hampstead. It cost a fortune to heat and I was skint. I kept the living room cold and we lived in the kitchen with the Rayburn. I used to turn the heater on in the bathroom 20 minutes before the kids were going to have their bath. It was miserable but I did four new plays in 1978: *The Singular Life of Albert Nobbs* with Susannah York, *An Audience Called Edouard* with Susan Hampshire and Jeremy Irons, *The London Cuckolds* with Ken Cranham and *Can You Hear Me at the Back?* with Hannah Gordon. All brilliant to do, but they didn't pay a lot. By the time I'd paid for childcare there was just enough to keep Eggy-in-the-Nest on our table.

In *Albert Nobbs*, Susannah and I played two 19th-century women who lived their lives as men in order to escape the crushing poverty that would usually have been a single woman's lot back then. It's a play about gender and inequality. I did it a year after Marilyn French's book *The Women's Room* came out. Once again I found myself involved in a percolating energy of the time. And I was living it: experiencing the impact of gender inequality at the hard end.

The fourth play I did that year, *Can You Hear Me at the Back?* had the most darling cast ever – Peter Barkworth, Hannah Gordon, Edward Hardwicke and Michael Maloney – but it was one of the worst plays ever. We toured for a few weeks and then brought it to the West End and spent a year at the Piccadilly Theatre. It was solid money but I didn't get the slightest bit of satisfaction from one performance.

I was working hard, always working; I was supporting my family but dragging myself along, in a deep depression. I called Peter Barkworth one day and told him I was just too low to do the performance that evening. He came round immediately.

'You have to do it, Stephie,' Peter warned me. 'The producers won't notice the difference if you're feeling off, but when the curtain goes up they'll notice if you're not there.'

Just after I'd co-starred in *The Nightcomers* with Marlon Brando, back in 1971, I'd failed to appreciate the power and influence producers have. I'd refused to do some publicity in New York. I was young, naive and didn't know how to deal with the different aspects of the business. It had resulted in the door to Hollywood being firmly shut in my face for a long time. Peter was a dear, wise man. It wasn't just the producers. I owed it to the cast to get myself together and go to work.

Despite the uninspiring nature of the play, it wasn't without its laughs. During one performance Peter managed to turn the line, 'I've watched you lose your nerve' to, 'I've natched you wooze your lerve.' He had me in fits on stage. I responded with 'Uh-huh' to which he replied, 'Oh, you beast.' We were playing. I badly needed to play. After another performance a young Canadian guy was waiting for me at the stage door. He came out with a line about 'falling in love with my back,' and asked me to a restaurant. To be in a situation where I'd have to talk was the last thing I wanted. I was so full of my story of misery I didn't dare go out to dinner. I told him to take me skating. He took me to the Electric Ballroom in Camden. It was perfect for me, a roller disco – no talking, just

*Left to right: Edward Hardwicke, Hannah Gordon and Michael Maloney
in my dressing room with Phoebe's paintings on the wall*

Peter Barkworth and me

all-night dancing on roller skates. I became a regular. It was one of a few clubs that played host to the black dance music scene in London at that time. After work I'd go dancing. I'd get home at daybreak, the music still pulsing through me and my body buzzing. When you totally lose yourself in the music, dancing induces its own kind of catharsis. It was what I needed: distraction – vibrant and intense distraction from my emotional pain. It was an unconscious recovery process and I became fit, in a head-turning kind of way. I discovered that if I didn't stop, if I kept on running, I could outpace the pain.

The process I'd use these days would be entirely different. I would try to sit with the pain. Far better to just sit with the pain; to let go of the fear, go through the pain and accept it as part of life at that moment. Back then I had to keep running for a long time. I didn't have a toolkit to draw on; I just kept on the move. On my 35th birthday I went hang-gliding on skis. I jumped off a cliff near Val d'Isère. I skied off the edge of the mountain thinking, 'If I die now, I'll die flying.'

While we were doing *Can You Hear Me at the Back?* I invited Michael Maloney to lodge with us. One day I asked him what he'd been doing earlier. He told me he'd been looking for a flat. I said, 'You're going to come into our house and be the big brother my girls need – the constant male.' I felt we needed that energy around the house. Michael was a 20-year-old macrobiotic of Jesuit schooling. He was the right person at the right time. Sent by the universe – as well as being opportunism of the highest order on my part. It's still how I live. Don't be shy – seize the moment.

I was lost in my own emotional state, as far as my own needs went, but I knew what my kids needed. It's because of them that I survived. My children made me brave.

There was only one time, when I saw them so happy with my mother and father, that I felt they'd be better off without me.

Soon after John and I separated I made a death dare. It wasn't a suicide attempt. I didn't decide to kill myself; I just didn't care about my life any more. I'd left Phoebe and Chloe with Granny and Gonky – as my father was called – and was driving back to London. They'd seemed so happy there. I thought that they'd be better off and happier if they lived with their grandparents permanently. My husband was already in another relationship and didn't need me. I thought everybody would be better off if I wasn't around. A lorry was driving towards me and I put destiny to the test. I switched to the other side of the road and drove head-on towards it, thinking, 'I'm not swerving.' It was a monstrously irresponsible thing to do. I am so lucky the driver of the lorry didn't go down the bank at the side of the road. For those seconds of idiocy I wasn't thinking. The lorry swerved and missed me.

For a few moments I stopped thinking, then I started thinking that if I did want to end the mess that was my life, I'd better tidy everything up. I got home and did just that. I tidied and tidied, and threw things away and tidied some more. When I'd finished, I thought, 'What a very neat house.' Then the children returned and went back to their nursery school, and I carried on. It's only later you realize that the thought of ending it all was not only an act of great selfishness but also an act of enormous foolishness, and totally misguided. Afterwards Mummy said to me, 'We were just putting on a brave face because we could see you were a bit glum.'

It seems so far away now, I feel as if I'm talking about a character in a novel. At the time, though, it was ghastly. The end of my marriage rent me apart. I couldn't conceive that this was the way my life was meant to be.

I wanted to brighten my bedroom so I bought some wallpaper decorated with roses. The thing is, I couldn't afford enough wallpaper to cover the whole room. I decided to cut the roses out and stick them on the walls. After I put the girls to bed I started cutting and sticking. Within an hour I'd given up. I felt exhausted – defeated. I started to weep. Suddenly Phoebe and Chloe were standing by me in their red jumpsuits.

'Why are you crying, Mummy?' Phoebe asked, her voice filled with concern.

'I'm not, honey,' I replied. 'I got wallpaper paste in my eyes.'

I pulled myself back to the here and now and, together, we started cutting and pasting. We made a great team: I cut, Phoebe pasted and Chloe slapped into place. We were up most of the night and we did the whole room. My children made me survive. For them, I had to be brave.

My favourite quote about having children is: 'Your children ruin your life and without them your life would have no purpose whatsoever.' I've always thought that my children were my greatest work of art, though with some of the things that have happened over the course of our lives together, I'm thankful I've also had my craft. Back then, they were my saviours.

Some people say you never get more than God knows you can cope with, and some say you are pushed to the very limit and always you will need help. And help *is* always there; your guardian angels, a higher power you can access. Towards the end of her life, when she was very frail, my mother was in the bath. She'd hit her head and was stuck. She didn't know how to get out. She said a prayer: 'Please God, help me to use my intelligence to get out of this bath.' In an instant, she had an answer. She pulled out the plug with her toe and, once the bath had drained, was able to get out. She was far too vain to push the emergency button, my mother.

Tenko

It was 1980 and a new decade was just beginning. I was having lunch with the great actor John Standing. He told me how he'd suddenly got the thought in his head that he'd like to go to India. He said the more he thought about it, the more appealing the idea of going there got. 'Then, the most extraordinary thing happened,' he continued. 'Out the blue I suddenly got a call saying could I possibly go out there – and now I'm going. I had

Old Camp Women (I'm front row, left)

this thought and then it happened.' I thought that was pretty cool, and wondered what *I* wanted. John gave me a concept and I flew with it. I don't think about things. I just do things.

I thought about myself in hot sunshine, being supported by the company of women. Maureen called me. The BBC was casting for a new drama series and my name had come up. The series was called *Tenko*. It was about a group of women interned in a Japanese camp in Singapore during the Second World War. There'd be just a couple of men in it. Initially, filming was happening on location in the Far East. Was I interested? I went for an interview with the producer Ken Riddington and the director Pennant Roberts. I let go and let God; visualizing myself glowing golden again, and with a very nice sun tan.

In terms of seniority of age, Jean Anderson came first. She played Jocelyn Holbrook. Jean was one of the greatest people you could ever wish to meet. She couldn't settle in the morning till she'd placed her bet for the 3:30 at Cheltenham that afternoon. That was Jean's thing. She was stalwart. I remember one time we were filming in the jungle and Pennant was doing a close-up of Jean. Her arm was supposedly broken, in a sling with a chair leg as a splint. As they were filming the close-up, with Jean standing, she started to move slowly out of frame, passing out stone-cold on the floor. The chair leg was too heavy, pulling down on the sling and constricting the veins in her neck. She'd fainted – and, of course, without complaining.

Next was Patty Lawrence – also, sadly, no longer with us. Patty played Sister Ulrica and she always had the best magazines – the ones that you wouldn't dare buy. Women's magazines like *Woman's Own*, *Woman's Realm*, *Women's Wear Daily* – they were heaven. A lot of advice was had from them and a lot of swapping went on. Patty was generous and wise, and she had one of the dearest husbands – Greville Poke.

Then there was Steph Cole. I was terrified of her. Steph played the rather stern Dr Beatrice Mason. It took me a bit of time to get to know her but she became a dear friend, who I still see. Ann Bell, who played Marion Jefferson, was a completely splendid leader of the women's camp with a wickedly wonderful sense of humour. Louise Jameson, who I call 'Miss Thesp', played Blanche Simmons. When we were filming *Tenko* there was only one thing wrong with Louise – her eyes were too blue. I used to make sure she wasn't wearing her blue contact lenses when we did scenes together. We've worked together since, in Moira Buffini's *Dinner*. She's a fabulous actress.

And then there was Veronica Roberts – someone I love as dearly as anyone on this planet. Ronnie played Dorothy Bennett. Louise pointed out, quite rightly, 'She's the wisest of us all, Stephie.' Ronnie is the most practical mix of spirituality and usefulness. I've often thought that if mankind was all composed of Ronnie, my sister Didi and my friend Patti Nicolella, I don't know that we'd build Brunel bridges but, my goodness, we'd build happy lives.

I had a dear friend who became celibate. When I asked her why she told me: 'Because I want to sleep with men I don't even want to have tea with.' As far as men were concerned, I felt that I was equally poor at making good choices. I thought it better I gave them a wide berth for a while. Women have a better facility for expressing their emotions and discussing things. They are grand company. I was so fortunate to land in a programme that was all women, and such quality women at that.

When John left me I was terrified the pain I felt would last forever. Now I know that pain is just a feeling and feelings come and go. They're part of the wonder of being. Being able to feel is one of the wonderful gifts of our embodiment in flesh. Other animals lick their wounds; they rest easy till they're mended. Accepting heartache, sitting with pain, hurts. We have a tendency to run. We try not to feel. We seek distraction and escape. John didn't ruin my life back then. The part of me that didn't feel I'd mucked it up myself allowed his behaviour to make me feel he'd ruined my life. But he hadn't. If I'd accepted that the pain I was feeling was the pain I was meant to be feeling and took responsibility for it, it would have passed far more quickly. But then I wouldn't have had the experience of those desperately bleak years in my life to learn from. For that I'm grateful.

God let Job suffer to test his faith. For a moment, driving home one night from my parents', my faith faltered. I was spared. God also let Job suffer in order to teach him humility. To let him know that none of us is beyond that essential ingredient to our miraculous being – pain. There really is no escaping it. Better to embrace it. Better to love it.

According to the Indian holy man Sri Nisargadatta Maharaj, our lives are a river flowing between the banks of pain and pleasure. Desire is the memory of pleasure, and fear the memory of pain. Both make us run, either towards or away. Both are essentially the same thing but wearing a different disguise. And both distract us from the absolute – love. There is no absolute truth other than this, and always so many ways of looking at things, as if through a prism. John had his reasons, and his own lessons to learn.

I used to think middle-aged people were so flaccid. I rather preferred the monstrous certainty of teenagers. People of middle-age and older seemed so noncommittal: 'Well, I really don't know.'

'What?! Why not? You should do – you're old enough.'

So many different ways of looking at it all, and no absolute truth apart from the fact that we really ought to be a little gentler with ourselves and with other people. Isn't that love shining through?

Burt Kwouk played Major Yamauchi, the man in *Tenko* in charge of the internment camp. He'd come in each day and bid us 'Good morning, ladies,' then walk over to his desk and stay out of our way till he was on set. We'd have little chats with him now and again during the day, but he let us decide when, and never tried to join the gang. He played the situation with sensitivity and tact.

Celebrity Big Brother

I used Burt Kwouk's example when I was left last woman standing during *Celebrity Big Brother* in 2010.

Twenty minutes before I was due to go into the house, I felt so underwhelmed and my spirits were low. I guessed it was fearfulness. Then I thought, 'I probably have every right to be afraid – I was about to enter car crash television.' Then I thought, 'OK, sweet girl, I dare you.'

Several days before, when I was making up my mind about whether or not to do it, I'd phoned a dear friend who's ex-SAS. You're not meant to say if you're SAS, and he hadn't, but I knew he was. He'd served in Ireland and the Gulf. I phoned him and just said, 'Hostage situation – give me a lecture on survival.'

And he did. Absolutely straight off, with no hesitation: 'Never volunteer and always support a weaker member of the group – it will empower you and it'll empower the group. Leave 20 seconds before you respond to anything and never respond with your first emotion. Find humour in everything; they're going to try to humiliate you and beat you down with whatever they can. If you find everything they do funny you can't be beaten and your spirit will stay intact.'

I couldn't have had more useful information. Especially when a cake descended on my head and I went and had a bath and cleaned up; only to be called back to have another cake descend on my head when I was clean, ready for bed and in my only pair of pyjamas. I managed to find it funny, when what they really wanted was for me to get completely furious because they'd just humiliated me. My friend's advice was invaluable.

The really fascinating thing about *Big Brother* was that it was very much like being in a convent. There was poverty, obedience and chastity. Well… chastity up to a point. When two members of the house decided to have sex in the bed opposite me, I took sleeping pills – which I had taken in on prescription. You had to make sure everything you thought you might need was on prescription; otherwise it wouldn't be allowed. I'd taken in prescription sunglasses to deal with the heavy lights, which were always on, and I was very thankful to have the sleeping pills. They meant I could avoid looking at, hearing or being annoyed with my two housemates for their sad tryst.

I snored that night, very loudly. The next morning, rather than being woken by the Joker's laugh, I heard what at first sounded like a whale, but turned out to be a magnified soundtrack of my own snoring. I laughed, apologized to everyone, and said, 'I'm so sorry. If you expel me from the house tomorrow, I will so understand.' But I didn't get expelled and ended up being the last woman standing. That snore became a ring tone you could download from eBay!

During that experience I discovered, under very difficult communal circumstances, that I was very happy being me; which was honestly, truly surprising. But I'd lived in a commune before; I knew all about sharing, and I have no problem with monastic existence. The whole thing was strangely spiritual. There was no reading allowed, but Stephen Baldwin, who's a deeply committed Christian, was allowed to have the Bible for an hour a day. We'd gather around and have Bible readings. They were fabulous. He was such a bad reader, though, I used to grab it from him and read out loud. Nicky, one of the girls, would say, 'Can we have something a bit nicer and not so preachy?' I'd say, 'I'm sure we can.' I read the Song of Solomon and the Book of Ruth; such fun and lovely chapters. I'd always known there are some fabulous things in the Bible. When Stephen left and the Bible was taken away, I cried. Some people put that down to a religious conversion, but I didn't need converting. I'd always known the Good Book was good.

Vinnie Jones was the alpha male and I was very conscious where I should put myself in relation to him; that I should align myself in second place, and that we should become mum and dad.

I didn't get into conflict with anyone, apart from one girl who was lazy – Lady Sov. I should have been more loving. The trouble was, she had absolutely no intention whatsoever to learn anything, but there you go.

One thing that really amused me was my being jealous of Ivana Trump coming into the house with two sets of sheets. They were 1,000 thread count percale cotton while the rest of us were sleeping in rather stiff acrylic. I was longing to nab a few sheets off her but I didn't, and we survived. Good girl, Ivana, hard worker; again, someone who's got a reputation. She used to be a Czechoslovakian Olympic skier. She's a grafter and I liked her a lot.

It felt very odd to sleep with four boys in the dormitory on the last couple of nights – very odd indeed. I wondered how best to deal with the situation and then I thought about Burt Kwouk. I remembered how he'd dealt with being the only man among all us girls on *Tenko*. I let the boys get on with their talking, and their boys-being-boys, and I kept myself to one side. I was the only girl in a group of boys and I didn't try to be Queen Bee. I was one of the boys when it was appropriate and kept myself to myself when it wasn't. *BB* turned out to be one of the great experiences.

Chapter Seven

In the Company of Women

Christina

In 1996 I was working with director Alan Dosser again, this
time on *No Bananas* for the BBC. The wonderful Alison
Steadman and I were playing sisters in wartime England.
Staying in London with my friend Christina Hart, I'd gone
out in the morning to get a manicure. We were filming that
afternoon. I had intended to be out all day, but completely on
impulse decided to go back. As I reached the house, I smelled
the wonderful smell of a log fire. I thought it a bit early in the
day for such comfort, but I registered it with pleasure. I entered
the house and was greeted by an overpowering smell of smoke.
I rushed upstairs to a blazing inferno. Christina's bedroom was
backdraft hell: curtains ablaze, desk, chairs and carpet − all
covered with six-foot jumping flames. Christina was in the bath.
Two minutes later and she would have been trapped. I dialled
911 then remembered where I was and dialled 999 instead. I

just managed to get the information over before the electricity cut out and the line went dead.

I got Christina and the cat out of the house and we waited for the fire engine while the windows turned black. Chaos ensued, and then we tramped through the debris, soot and damp, to examine the damage. The firefighters were wonderful. Neighbours, with sweet tea, arrived and gathered and I had five minutes to get to work. I went into my bedroom in a cold frame of mind and packed all my sooty belongings into black bags. My taxi arrived and a dishevelled and grubby actress got into the cab and said, 'The nearest dry cleaners please.' The laundry man must have thought Christmas had come early as I counted through the garments. I threw the sooty bags away and, with hair and clothes smelling like smoked kippers, went to join the film unit and turn up for work. My nails would have to wait.

I first met Christina in 1977, four weeks after Chloe was born. John had made a film with Christina's husband, David. We went to dinner at their house. David was a great character. Christina, me and our kids have remained solid and constant ever since. Our relationship has been extraordinary. Very sadly, David died of motor neurone disease at the beginning of 2011.

David had bought the most glorious estate in Suffolk called Coldham Hall. It was totally in its original state. The summer he bought it, Christina, her sons Nicky and Timmy, Phoebe, Chloe and I went to stay there. We set up a very basic kitchen in a room that wasn't going to be the kitchen and had an adventure, camping in a haunted mansion. The 17th-century owners of Coldham Hall had provided the horses that had been used in the Gunpowder Plot. Its history is steeped in Catholic intrigue.

When we moved in, the building hadn't been lived in for ages. There wasn't a stick of furniture and the planned renovations hadn't started. We explored from top to bottom, uncovering old and forgotten priest holes as we went. There was no electricity so we had to use candles for light. It was all very spooky.

There was a chapel in the Hall, and in another room two portraits of a pair of nuns hung on the wall. Someone came to take them away for a clean up. They dropped the hammer they were using to take them off the wall; it smashed a bowl. Then they fell off their ladder. Legend had it that if the portraits were ever removed from the Hall, there would be trouble. The nuns didn't want to go.

I decided to have some fun with the spirits. I made a Ouija board by arranging the letters of the alphabet around the edge of a plate, with a knife in its centre. We were using it one night when the knife started spelling out words in a mad way. Suddenly a bat flew out of the fireplace. It darted really low over one of the candles, knocking it onto the plate. As far as we knew, the chimneys were all blocked. It was terrifying. The spirits didn't want to play. The whole house was haunted. Up till then we'd been sleeping in different rooms: Christina with her children, and me with mine. That night we all huddled together.

I was trying to shake the spirit tree to see what would happen. I knew there was life after death and I knew there were ghosts in Coldham Hall. I saw one, turning a corner and disappearing through a shut door. It was another version of reading the children a scary bedtime story. There was no permanent damage. Children love to be frightened and then to know everything is warm and cosy and Mum's made hot chocolate. But on some of those nights we cuddled up very tight.

A malevolent spirit followed us back to London. We were in the fast lane from Suffolk when the car suddenly conked out. As I tried to get over to the hard shoulder I told everyone that if they believed in God they'd better pray now. God got us safely over, just.

Pammy

There were more friends and more women in my life. There were two sisters: Brenda, who lived in London, and her sister Pammy, who lived on Dartmoor.

The house Pammy leased on the moor was very important to us. I put a roof on it, replacing the 'Dartmoor thatch' (the corrugated iron). I should have kept the house when Pammy moved, but the moor claims back to itself, and to the wild, very fast. You really have to be living there.

Dartmoor is very healing. The land is rich in quartz. It's no surprise it's host to fairies and pixies and magic. It's a spiritual place, a great place for mending, and the place I've laughed more than anywhere else on God's green earth. I could recount endless adventures but none that are much more than struggling across the moors carrying cornflakes, brought because there was nothing in the local shop, and eating an odd diet of fresh vegetables, which you've managed to stop the Dartmoor ponies from poaching, and geese eggs – because geese make the best guard dogs.

It's where I taught the children to ride, if you can call donkey-riding proper riding. There was Rupert the donkey as well as Odin the horse and various ponies, but Rupert was the steed of

Christina and baby at Coldham

The house on Dartmoor

choice. Rupert would stand very still until you put a hat on him. If you put any old hat on him, he'd walk. If you wanted him to go any faster you'd have to put an Australian cork hat on him. Then he'd start trotting; he liked the action of the corks.

Dartmoor was simplicity itself, and very basic living. There was no hot running water; in fact, no running water in the house at all for the first 15 years we were there. There was no electricity, just gas. Then the generator arrived. The trouble with generators is that you're forever spending hours, usually in the rain, mending them. One of my greatest pleasures always was to take a bowl of water that I'd heated on the Aga and, never mind the weather, strip off outside and wash in the moonlight. There's great beauty in washing really simply. Like everything else, the loo was very basic: past the vegetable patch, down the garden in a little shed with a little hole – that was it. The house on Dartmoor was the perfect place just to be.

Imagine this: the River Dart is down below, twinkling. You're standing in the garden of the cottage. There's a pony, there's a horse, there's a donkey and there are geese – and you are in heaven. You've made your way through the farmyard, the farm gate and the sheep dip. You'd driven up over the moors, and where the car got stuck is where the car will stay until you try to dig it out in a few days' time. You've unloaded the car and, because it's dark, walked towards the lights of Princetown. Then, following the lights of the prison you get to the stone shepherd's cottage. When you arrive, you open the back door. You're greeted by chickens and, yes, they do live inside and, frankly, the only clean place is Odin's stable, because he's the hero of everything. Being a mighty horse, he's kept immaculate. Everything else is

Dartmoor shambles. But the sheets are of the finest linen, and the comforters are pure down, because they were bought in a sale at a great house.

Pammy was once snowed in for six weeks. She heard the helicopter and when she saw that it was the Army coming to rescue her she thought she'd better give them a proper welcome. She stripped down and put on her suspender belt and stockings, no doubt laddered, and her lift-up bra. She opened the door in her underwear, saying, 'Nice to see you boys.'

Dartmoor was fine alternative living; the continuation of my fabulous hippie days. Pammy lives in New Zealand now with her husband, the poet Cliff Fell. She used to live with another dear friend who was called Hairy Pete. When they moved to Dartmoor his name changed to Fairy Pete.

It wasn't until Pammy was seven months along that she realized she was pregnant with her last baby. When she found out, she phoned me and asked if I would put a phone in at the Dartmoor house. 'They say I can't have the baby on the moors unless I've got a telephone,' she told me. 'Of course I'll put one in,' I assured her. That's the only reason she was the slightest bit interested in having one. Before then, arrivals had always been forewarned telepathically, and were usually a day or so in or out.

Dartmoor is a haven in my heart and I can go there at any time. When my grandmother was very old and living in a care home, I asked her what she did all day. She looked up at a picture hanging on the wall. 'I go there,' she answered. Just as my grandmother had lived in her picture, after she was moved from her sweet bungalow with her budgerigar and roses to an old people's home, I can go to that sweet cottage on Dartmoor.

In every cell of my body I can smell the wood smoke, hear the laughter, feel the good living and taste the often very erratic food – because we'd often run out of stuff.

Pammy once tricked me. I was on my way out and hammering down the stairs. 'There's a lamb in the oven, Stephie,' Pammy called out to me. I was about to say 'Oh, yummy' and then I thought, 'Hang on, she's a vegetarian.' I opened the bottom oven in the range and there was a little baby lamb. Its mother had died in the night and Pammy had found it. At the time I only ever wore white. The lamb thought that I was its mummy. I've never been able to eat lamb since. I can eat an old mutton but that baby, with its tiny tail and little legs that it could hardly stand on, put me off for life.

So many parties, so much fun, so much sharing. There was no money at all involved in that existence. The rent was £2 a week. And suddenly, when it looked as if the lease from the Duchy might get discontinued, Pammy did what only Pammy would do. She managed to duck under the cordons, get past the police and run to where Prince Charles was getting out of a helicopter. There were lots of photographers there waiting to snap the prince and they got Pammy. 'I hear you've got a lot of sway around here,' she said to him. Her story got told and the lease on the cottage was renewed. I think I've inspired her and I know she's inspired me, and her sister Brenda, too. They're like family.

Sometimes, if I've had a bad day or before I go into the studio, if I know the work's going to be a challenge, I'll take myself on a guided meditation to one of the places I carry in my heart: Dartmoor, Coldham, Malibu. Or I just look out of the window and find a scene of normal life going on outside. Sometimes I'm lucky and it's a cricket match or a football game being played by kids. I take it in and think that these people, going about their lives, playing their game, are totally unruffled by what I'm going through. So it's not that important and it will pass. Soon I, too, will be part of that normal life and fun and games again; very soon. Then I go into my tunnel and get on with the task.

Didi

My sister Didi told me that one night lying in her bed when she was 16 she said a prayer: 'Please, dear God, don't ever let me be jealous of Stephie.' That evening I'd come home after winning a jiving competition with a boy that she really liked. God's never let her.

Didi does a good job with everything she puts her hand to. When she's finished she just says, 'There you are, if you want more then get it yourself.'

She and I know how to have the best time ever, over a cup of tea, with both of us hysterical on the sofa. We once had a phone call where not one word was said; we had the giggles for three-quarters of an hour. Best medicine. Didi just enjoys life and she appreciates the good things. As our mother used to, she'll raise a glass of water to her lips: 'The elixir of life,' she'll say. She's been my greatest source of encouragement. Whenever I say, 'I'm going to give all this up,' she says, 'No, you can't, I enjoy being famous.' I've been happy to take her all over the world with me.

My sister Didi, supporting me

When I was filming *A Change of Place* in Budapest in 1994, I had it written into my contract that Didi would be accompanying me. When I was leaving, CBS, one of the television companies involved in producing the film, asked Didi if she'd stay on because they'd enjoyed her company so much. They even offered to pay her. 'No,' she told them, 'but I've had a lovely time, thank you.' Didi just does what needs to be done.

She and I both live in America. Didi saw me when I was first on the front cover of the listings magazine *TV Guide* when nobody in the UK did. I realized I wasn't as thrilled as I could have been and I wondered why. I realized it was because Mummy wouldn't be buying a copy. Didi was there to see it, though.

Emily

When you become well known you get fans, but you never know what your fans expect of you. When I was doing *An Ideal Husband* in 2001 at the Paper Mill Playhouse in New Jersey, a girl turned up at the stage door after a performance. I think I signed a photograph for her. She said she'd been longing to meet me and that she'd come all the way from Ohio. We chatted a bit and that was that. I finished the production, went back to Los Angeles and then, suddenly, she turned up in the condominium building in West Hollywood where I had an apartment and made friends with my daughter Phoebe.

I had to have a bit of a think about that. She invited Phoebe into her apartment. The walls were covered with photographs of me. 'This could be worrying,' I thought. Having an obsession like that made me think she was probably unhappy and had problems in her life. Phoebe let her babysit Jude. I thought I'd better get to know her. I realized I had a decision to make. She had an image of me based on the fantasy characters she'd seen me play. I knew I was more than that and figured I probably had nothing to worry about. Anyway, I had nothing to hide. She seemed very bright and was obviously very efficient and organized. She knew everything about my career and remembered it all far better than I did.

I decided not to be anxious or swayed by fear. She wasn't in a happy state when we first met. She'd been through some terrible experiences in her life. I saw into her, I saw her need, not her adoration of a fantasy of me. I decided to hold on to what I saw with love, albeit at a distance. I could have been really worried; I could have reported her to the police. I could have said, 'There's a girl who has photographs of me all over the place, and it's really worrying me.'

That was ten years ago. Since then, I've seen Emily through the death of her mother, and through the death of her father. She looks after my house and my dogs while I'm away. She's my assistant when I'm in America.

When I started *Tenko* I'd been so very unhappy and those women gave me so much. We saw each other's needs and supported one another. That experience helped me recognize Emily's needs and I warmed to her. It's quite interesting what you can do once you've recognized whether it's love or fear that's guiding your decisions.

Maria

Being in the company of Maria Callas while I was playing at being her for the play *Master Class* for several months in 2010-11 was quite a challenge. She was a formidable woman. What David Beckham was to football, Maria Callas was to opera. Her peers were stunned by her ability; they really believed that she'd been touched by the gods, and that she radiated a divine energy in her voice. But she suffered terribly. She didn't have a happy childhood and, as an adult, was hit by one scandal after another. *Master Class* is set at the end of her career, and of her life. She died when she was 54.

When we took the play to Edinburgh we performed at the same theatre that she'd performed in 53 years before we were there. She'd been contracted by La Scala, the famed opera house in Milan, to do four performances of *La Sonnambula*. The management had then tacked on two more performances, which she'd refused to do. She was vocally exhausted and had to get back to Venice for a party arranged for her by Elsa Maxwell, the original celebrity gossip columnist. La Scala were furious. Ghiringhelli, who ran La Scala, sacked her.

When I did the play in Edinburgh, all sorts of weird things happened. During one performance I felt Maria Callas come on stage while I was at the point in the play where I am explaining to a student (beautifully played by Robyn North) how to approach playing *La Sonnambula*. Maria started gabbling in my ear in Greek, just as I was in the middle of a soliloquy. I wanted to slap her but there was nothing physical there to slap. It was terrible. It wasn't like she came and suddenly empowered me. She just gabbled in Greek, right into my ear. It was most off-putting. Then I saw a curtain move up in the box known as the director's box. 'That's Ghiringhelli,' I thought. It wasn't ghostly. I was too busy to let it make me shiver. To top it all, I lost my voice. In 45 years I'd never lost my voice before. I could growl and I could squeak, but there was nothing in the middle. I had to miss the last two performances. I was distraught at letting everyone down, but in that wonderful old theatre, channelling that diva, it was strangely perfect.

Chapter Eight

Dying and Coming Back

Near Death

I was playing Aquilina opposite Ian McKellen's Pierre in Thomas Otway's *Venice Preserv'd* at the National Theatre in 1984. I'd come off stage and was removing my make-up because I had to get to the hospital. I'd promised I'd be there before 11 o'clock and had arranged to have a drink with the rest of the cast before going because we had a ten-day break from the show. I was rushing.

Suddenly, I was hit by a terrible premonition. A feeling of imminent catastrophe washed over me and the thought gripped me; 'Oh no, this is going to go really, really wrong.'

The play's director, Peter Gill, was already in the Green Room.

'I'm really not feeling good about this,' I told him.

'Well of course you're not,' he replied. 'You're going to hospital to have an operation.'

'I think it's more than that,' I said.

'Ahhh, you'll be fine,' he tried to convince me.

'I won't be,' I thought.

Ian came in. 'I'm not feeling good about this,' I told him.

'You'll be *fine*, my dear.' He does that reassuring thing very naturally.

Well, whatever. 'Bye folks, see you in ten days' time.'

I put it out of my mind and got to the Royal Free. The nurse was cross. It was nearly 11 o'clock, I'd just come off stage and now I had to get into bed and pretend to be ill. I wasn't ill. I was just there for a necessary operation.

Everyone else on the ward was asleep. I think I managed to have a shower. The nurse showed me a mangy little bed in the corner. 'Everyone's going to bump into it as they walk by,' I thought. It had a flimsy curtain round it. 'Not nice digs.'

I was on the main ward: low rank, no privileges. No problem. I wasn't staying there long. I had ten days to have the operation and recover, then back to work.

The morning after surgery I painted my toenails, replaced my jewellery and started working on designs for our new house. By day three my temperature was spiking to 104 degrees and I was feeling very poorly. I was moved to a private room with en suite loo, an emergency button and a wonderful view of the whole of Hampstead Heath – special privileges. I was moving fast up the ranks. The problem was I was very ill.

The situation quickly unravelled. Having vomited green bile in a dramatic splash against the wall opposite the window, I turned to look at the clouds but I couldn't hold focus. I was fading, becoming part of the clouds. I was floating. No longer in pain, I was looking down on my body lying in a messy bed. I was floating on the ceiling of a white hospital room observing slippers on the floor, books piled on the side locker and myself, lying blank-faced on the bed in a white nightdress.

There was a jump-cut to another scene. I don't know how it happened – it just did. I was being led down a wide, rough path towards a boulder; behind it was the most beautiful, warm and inviting golden light. I was being led by four Franciscan monks. I think that's what they were. They were to my left, wearing very coarse, brown, woven habits with hoods, as in images of St Francis of Assisi. Their hoods were up so I couldn't see their faces. Their habits were tied with thick rope belts and they wore sandals. Not of our time but also not frightening – not at all. Not even strange. The scene was welcoming. I knew the light was God and that the boulder was the stone of Jesus' tomb. I was aware that I was leaving *and* arriving; that I was going away from the pain and coming home.

Chloe's eyes

Suddenly two enormous eyes, like those of a huge owl, swooped in and filled my entire field of vision. I recognized them as my daughter Chloe's eyes, and they were saying, 'Oh, no, you don't!'

Then, like a film going backwards, everything rewound and I found myself back in the hospital bed. I managed to press the emergency button, which remarkably was still in my hand, and set off the red lights and bells. A doctor rushed in and started fussing around. I said to her, 'I think I just died.'

Without missing a beat she replied, 'Yes, I think you probably did.'

I was rushed into theatre for emergency surgery. They couldn't get hold of anyone in my family to sign me off, but Steph Cole came up and signed. Pretty ironic, really – in *Tenko* her character had suffocated mine with a pillow as a mercy killing at my character's request.

It was late on a Saturday night and a surgeon had to come from St Thomas' Hospital. He looked so dapper in his bow tie I made him breathe over me so I could check if he'd been drinking. Having come back, I didn't want to be killed off a second time.

I came round after the operation to a hazy consciousness, bandaged like a mummy and with tubes everywhere. I drifted for days; fed through a drip and filled with 12 different antibiotics to kill the infection that had nearly killed me.

I was down to 90lb but, until my gut worked again, I was not allowed to eat anything. I had cheated one night with the pith of a cherry, and regretted it for hours afterwards – the pain was terrible. The next day they were going to operate and fit a colostomy bag. It would be permanent. They tried to reassure me that I'd be able to live with it but the thought was horrific.

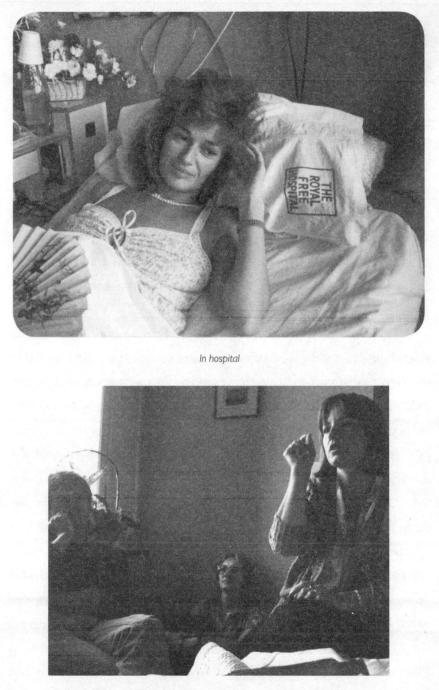

In hospital

Aiding my recovery. Left to right: Martyn, Leigh and Ronnie

Dear Ronnie Roberts saved me. She took over my room with her girlfriend Leigh and Martyn Stanbridge, my young companion at that time.

'This is what we're going to do, sweet girl,' she told me. 'We're going to say a prayer and I'm just going to work on your tummy and I promise I won't hurt you.' Ronnie got me to imagine a tiny paralysed kitten, a little wounded creature, inside my belly. She had Leigh on one of my feet and Martyn on the other, gently manipulating the acupressure points that stimulate the intestines. Barely touching me she worked her healing magic, drawing light circles with the gentlest of touch on my stomach. During that night I passed wind. Everything had joined up again and I didn't have to have a colostomy.

Ronnie is so spiritual and also so practical. Isn't that the way it's meant to be? The practical and the spiritual are not mutually exclusive. You can turn washing-up into a spiritual task. You can fold the clothes, definitely bathe a baby and you can help a friend, with practical spirituality.

John came to visit me when I was still very poorly. I was also a filthy mess. He asked me if I needed anything.

'Yes! I need a bath. I need to wash my hair. Look, it's got bile in it. The most the nurse will do is pat me with a wet flannel.'

He gathered my wraith-like body in his arms and carried me to the bathroom, somehow wheeling the drip stand I was connected to alongside us. He stripped me bare, covering the bandages wrapped around my stomach with a nurse's apron, and proceeded to wash my hair and bathe me in the shower. I was like a limp rag doll in his hands. He washed me gently, until I was clean. There was only one person I knew who would have done such a mad thing. That was John.

Beach hair

Best hair

With The Colbys cast
Left to right: John James, Emma Samms,
Charlton Heston, Barbara Stanwyck, me

Chuck and me

With Luke Perry, my son in Beverley Hills, 90210

Glamour Puss

With Christopher Cazenove in To Be The Best, *Hong Kong*

Christina Hart

With Col: 'Control' and 'Judgement' on a good day

With my parents in Somerset

Lindsay Wagner and me, on a slow boat to China

Bernie, doctor and musician

With partner Vincent Simone in Strictly Come Dancing 2007 – not my finest hour

With Bill Roache

At home with Nutrina and Sienna (photographed by Judy Geeson)

Connie

My agent Maureen came to see me with a thick stack of scripts. 'This is what we've been waiting for' she said, and plonked them on the bed.

'Oh, Maureen that's too heavy, I can't take any weight on the sheet.'

She put them on the side table.

'Read through them when you can,' she said on her way out.

I couldn't show any interest. Work seemed a long way away. I was weak and felt barely alive. Later, I needed a tissue. Maureen had put the scripts on top of my box of tissues. To get to the box I had to move the pile, and I only had the strength to lift one script at a time. I lifted the first one and it was so much effort I thought, 'Now I've got it in my hand I might as well read it.' Once I'd started, I couldn't stop. I read the whole night. I read through the entire series of 13 episodes. It was brilliant, it was mine, and I had to do it.

The script was for a television series called *Connie*. It was about a woman returning to the UK to take back control of her family's ailing business after living in Greece. Connie was a grafter. She was a survivor. She was a trickster. I liked her immediately. I knew her character could mend me. I knew I could use her to obliterate the sadness from my life once and for all. By entering the world of this formidable and courageous woman I could bring about my own recovery.

The trouble was I had to get the part. I phoned Alan Dosser, the director, and said, 'She's mine.' He asked for a meeting and I lied that I was down at my parents' house in Somerset, had not been very well and didn't want to come to London, hoping we could just do it on the phone.

'That's fine,' he said, 'I'm coming to the West Country next week.' So I discharged myself from the Royal Free, promising my doctors I would arrange to continue the intravenous antibiotics by daily injections, which turned out to be like being injected with an icing syringe.

A friend arranged a private ambulance and I beat Alan to the West Country by a couple of days.

My mother offered me her complete backing. 'Darling, I can't believe how determined you are to recover,' she told me. 'Whatever you decide to do, I will support you, totally.' She couldn't believe I'd survived. She'd probably been thinking I'd die and she'd have to bring up Phoebe and Chloe.

Martyn and Mummy arranged me in a deck chair outside the beach hut. Once I was sitting, that was it. I couldn't move. I was so ill. I still wasn't much more than a wraith, so Mummy put padding in my bra. I couldn't let Alan see what kind of state I was in. Martyn had to take care of the tea. I told him just to offer and to be aware of everything without making me boss him about. I had it all very carefully stage-managed. Alan was an anarchist, a risk-taker. He's wickedly good news. He'd been artistic director at the Liverpool Everyman and was used to sailing close to the edge. Still, there was no way I wanted him to know the state I was in.

The meeting was going very well and the conversation was flowing. Then I got rather excited about something Alan was saying. I forgot myself momentarily and thought I'd stretch my legs on the white picket fence in front of me. I lifted one leg and put it on the fence. It took all my energy. I couldn't lift my other leg to join it, and remained in that ungainly position for the rest of the meeting.

Connie: another life, anoth...

She was going to bring me back to...

It was the middle of the secon...

weak.

'Alan,' I said, out of everyone els...

don't think I'm going to be able to do thi...

'I understand – that's OK,' he repli... ...a

beat, he continued, 'Do you want to stop ... ...you want

to carry on blocking out the scenes so we've got it blocked for

anyone who might take over till the end of the day?'

I told him I'd keep going and at the end of the day he said,

'See you tomorrow.' It was just a little moment.

Connie was so fabulous. Ron Hutchinson's concept for *Connie*

had been based around the political question of whether or

not it was possible for a single businesswoman to make it in

Thatcher's Britain and maintain her integrity, without 'old

money' or becoming involved in corruption. It was a very

pertinent question and right on the mark at the time but, set in a

knitting factory in the Midlands, I was concerned it wouldn't be

glamorous enough to attract a large audience. I thought we might

dress it up a bit.

'What's the American programme that's on at the moment?'

I asked Alan. 'You know the one – *Dynasty*.' We glamorized *Connie*

in a way that had never been intended. I was pulling *Dynasty*, like

a set, towards me.

At one point in the series Connie admits herself to hospital.

I'd already had the full training. The intravenous acting I was

doing for *Connie* came straight out of the Royal Free. I had

hobbling-with-an-IV acting down to a tee.

...ront of my mind was one over-arching question: ...ived, why had I come back?

Once again I was aware that there was so much more to everything than the three dimensions our lives appear to take place in. On a physical level I knew *Connie* was going to be amazingly difficult – I'd been so ill – but it felt like a blessing, an opportunity I'd been handed on a plate. My agent Maureen's words, 'It's what we've been waiting for,' echoed through my mind.

On the first day of filming we shot a scene where Connie hijacks a car. She arrives at the airport from Greece and has to get into town. She gets into a car with a chauffeur. We were waiting to do the next shot. I was in the back seat, when out of the blue – 'I've got a couple of messages for you,' the chauffeur said, looking at me in the rear view mirror.

'Oh?' I wondered what he was talking about.

'You've been incredibly ill and have had two operations.'

'Sorry?' I replied, stunned. I knew that he hadn't been told anything, because nobody we were working with knew I'd been ill. He turned around to face me.

Seeing the shock on my face, he apologized. 'I'm sorry… my wife and I run the Psychic Society of Great Britain. A couple of messages came through for you last night.'

'Oh really?' I said.

'One is that you are to drop all hate and all thought of retribution for what happened to you, because it won't aid you in your mending.'

'Oh, and by the way,' the chauffeur continued, 'you needn't worry about money because you're never going to have to want for that. The other message I've got for you is that you can mend your scars with spring green and spring yellow. Those are the healing colours you should meditate on.'

How would he know I had scars? There was no way he could have known. Meditating on spring green and spring yellow really did work – my scar is barely visible.

I always get three estimates for any work that needs doing. Just before and during rehearsals I'd gone to see three psychics, separately. I didn't tell any of them about what had happened. I didn't mention the fact that I'd been ill. I just went and asked for a reading. Each of them said the same thing – virtually word for word. They told me that I'd been through a major event and that the focus now would be to find my own spiritual truth. They said that during the first half of my life I had lived very physically, and that the second half would be lived spiritually. There were no vitamins to take, no exercises to do. I just took it on board, said 'thank you,' and got on with what I was doing.

I had no idea what their readings meant. At the time it didn't really make sense. I laughed cynically when, not so long after, I got offered work in Hollywood, thinking, 'Oh yes, not much physicality there.' Of course, I didn't know that Southern California is a feast of all spirituality.

From the point I nearly died, the universe opened up for me. God's divine munificence began to become very apparent. *Connie* was the first gift. What the chauffeur told me made total sense: drop the hate, drop the story, drop the pain, drop all that stuff and let the gold shine through.

Connie was filmed in Nottingham during the miners' strike. It was a very harsh time. I always seem to find myself in the right place – witnessing events from the front seat. I felt it on the streets of Nottingham. The pawn shops were overflowing: diamond rings, tea sets, right down to sheets and pillow cases people were forced to pawn. Those were hard, hard times.

Then, suddenly, I was there on the other side. I was present at a lunch for one of Thatcher's speech writers. Reagan's speech writer was there, too, along with other people from the world of politics.

Our host was raising a large slice of rare roast beef, impaled on a fork.

'Are those miners being allowed to stop paying their mortgages while they're on strike?' he asked.

'Yes, I think so,' somebody answered.

'Right,' he said, blood and gravy spilling over his lips. 'We've got them; we'll force them to pay.'

I worked with some fabulous people on *Connie*, including the wonderful Pam Ferris. She's a real roll-up-your-sleeves-and-get-on-with-the-job type of person – a great joy to work with. Pam played Connie's step-sister Nester. I remember being in the make-up room watching her on the monitor: 'Whoa, she's like a tank, she is so strong.' I was still recovering and nowhere near back up to weight. I suddenly saw Pam as a rhinoceros. If she was a rhinoceros, I wondered what I should be. I wondered what animal could beat a rhinoceros. It dawned on me: I'd be a fox.

I thought of Renaud the Fox standing up on his hind legs, laughing and taunting that rhinoceros so badly that it charges full force and then, at the very last moment, stepping out of the way and letting the rhinoceros impale its horn and get stuck. That's how you beat a rhinoceros. I'd worked out how Connie was going to beat Nester. I was so thin and tiny and Pam was big and angry and strong. I kept that image of the rhinoceros and the fox in my mind, because Nester was one of Connie's primary adversaries.

When I was working on *The Colbys* I was very conscious that Sable was a panther. It's hard to run faster than a panther, and they know how to laze extremely gracefully, with claws in or out. Sable was a panther. Connie was a fox. I use animal imagery a lot.

Peter Straker was one of my other co-stars on *Connie*. I called him 'the Minister of Entertainments'. I'd known Peter since the days of *Hair*, back in the Sixties. He's an enchanting, lovely man and a dear friend. It was through Peter that I met one of the

Peter Straker and me

most entrancing people who ever was – Freddie Mercury. When we met, Freddie and I had an immediate bond. He came to see me a few years after *Connie* had finished, when I was in *The Rover* in 1988. Afterwards, Freddie took me to Steph's Restaurant on Dean Street for supper. I think we both recognized in each other that the private person and public person are very different. I treasure having known Freddie, even though it was for a sadly short time.

Chapter Nine

California Dreaming

The girls and I had gone to stay in Somerset. It was summer, 1985. *Connie* was in the can.

I was mended. We'd gone down to the sea the same day we'd arrived at my parents' house. I was standing on the deck in front of the beach hut. Suddenly, a vision – I could see red-tiled roofs and a palm tree. And the thought – 'God's going to send me to California, how extraordinary.' Just like that: the vision and the thought, together. I didn't connect it to anything. It didn't relate to anything I was aware of. I didn't think about it beyond its own simple and self-contained scene.

My next door neighbour in London was looking after the house while we were away, watering the plants and feeding the fish. She'd locked herself out. The fish were getting hungry and the plants were thirsty. The phone rang. I thought it was her again. It was Maureen.

'Something's come up – you may be interested. Can you be back in London the day after tomorrow?' she asked.

The producers of *Dynasty* were auditioning for a role in another series they were producing. Funny – I'd used the programme as inspiration to inject a bit of glamour into *Connie*. I really wasn't that keen; I thought they were probably after some

American star. Still, it was an opportunity to get into our house, save the fish from starving and re-hydrate the plants.

'OK, I'll come,' I told Maureen. 'Just for the afternoon – I am on holiday, you know.' Maureen couriered the audition piece to me and I took it to the beach. Before I'd had the chance to have a proper look, the wind grabbed it. It landed in the sea. I laughed. I wasn't particularly bothered, but I went up to London. When I arrived at the studio where they were taping the auditions, I noticed a sharp tang of adrenaline and perspiration hanging in the air. People had been nervous. This was a big deal; people wanted this desperately. I picked up a script someone had left behind. 'I'm going for this,' I thought. A couple of days later, back in Somerset, the phone rang. It was Maureen. The producers wanted to see me in Los Angeles. I was going to Hollywood.

Hollywood

Getting the part of Sable Colby depended on an interview with Aaron Spelling, the executive producer of *Dynasty*. He'd produced all the most popular TV shows since the 1970s, and *Dynasty* was no exception. Since it had first aired in 1981 it had been a huge hit. Audiences dressed up and had *Dynasty*-watching parties.

I was shown into his office. It was very large and there was an ocean of thick shag carpet I had to wade through – very difficult to accomplish elegantly – before reaching an enormous desk behind which was a small, slim, suntanned Texan with white hair and a sweet smile.

'You're younger than I thought you'd be,' he said.

'But much more experienced,' I countered. I wanted this. You can't pay school fees for two daughters on the wages from the National Theatre.

The conversation went back and forth for a few more rounds, Aaron's voice a soft Texan twang, and then he lifted a large white telephone and said, 'I'm sending her to wardrobe.' It was straight out of the movies. Within minutes I was being measured by the great designer Nolan Miller and Sable was being brought to life.

I was back in Hollywood after a 15-year gap.

While we were both working on the Hammer film *Dracula AD 1972*, I became friends with Marsha Hunt. It was Marsha's afro on the poster for the musical *Hair*.

The year after we did the film together we went to the States, taking Karis, the daughter she'd had with Mick Jagger, to visit all her family. I was the 'honky rep', Marsha said, to prove to her middle-class family that not all white people were dishonest

With Marsha Hunt and Christopher Lee on the set of Dracula AD 1972

and lazy. We started on the West Coast and then went to the East Coast. I then went on to New York and stayed in the penthouse of the Sherry Netherland Hotel at the invitation of the owner, who'd had to leave town but said I could stay 'until Tuesday week, when Jacqueline Kennedy will be staying. Please don't eat the ice cream in the freezer, it's her favourite.'

While I was there I bumped into one of producers who had worked on *The Nightcomers*. He'd just sold the film to the legendary producer Joseph E. Levine, and invited me to meet him. When we met, Joseph E. suggested I do some publicity for the film, since I was in the States. He said he could get me on *The Johnny Carson Show* the following day. The idea terrified me. I was taken by surprise – suddenly caught on the back foot. I didn't think I had the right clothes with me to do publicity, and my hair would need styling. I felt flustered and totally unprepared.

'How about *Playboy*?' he asked. 'If you agree to *Playboy* I can absolutely guarantee you an Oscar nomination.'

'I couldn't do that!' I exclaimed.

'Why not? You were naked in the film!'

'That was different. I was in character then.'

'I don't understand why you won't co-operate?'

'I just can't agree to any of this,' I said.

The irritation was rising in his voice. 'This is how it works here and, believe me, if you leave this room with that attitude, you are dead in this business!'

I got up and started to leave.

'Ever seen a skeleton dance?' I said as I walked through the door.

Big mistake – he was true to his word. I was blacklisted

in Hollywood. A few months later Sam Pekinpah told me he'd wanted to test me for *Straw Dogs* but the studio wouldn't let him. I was young, naïve, fearful and feeling insecure, but I'd come over as arrogant and cocky. I could have told him I needed an outfit and a hairdresser. He would have been only too delighted to have sorted out those details for me. I didn't know how to ask for things like that back then. I didn't know how it all worked.

I also didn't have the confidence to be able to appear as 'me', rather than as a character. I used to find publicity impossibly embarrassing. I didn't realize the value of it; that it had to be done. I was quite shy. I found it very hard to face the public as Stephanie Beacham. I didn't understand the system. I believed in 'Art'. I distrusted anyone who wore a suit and I didn't realize that producers are the most important people in any business – without them there wouldn't be any work.

It was fear that stopped me. I was frightened. I was uncooperative out of fear. When I was younger, because of my deafness, I'd always taken the arrogant road to cover up the fact that I couldn't hear very well. I'd pretend I was bored – it was a pose, a front. I used it now and it was my undoing. It's much better just to be truthful.

The crazy thing is I actually did pose for *Playboy* the following year. I did it out of wickedness or stupidity, or both. It cost me $1,000,000. I was in Jamaica on holiday and *Playboy* phoned up – don't know how they found me. I simply said, 'I will if you can get Litchfield or Snowdon here by tomorrow,' and put the phone down. And they did. Patrick fell off the plane the next morning. But they kept the pictures back and didn't use them. Then, just when I'd made a splash in *The Colbys*, and was being portrayed as this elegant creature, to the embarrassment of my children the pictures hit the stands. They lost me the $1,000,000 cosmetics contract I'd had lined up. It did give me the opportunity to tell my girls that they could do whatever they wanted in their lives, but that there were always repercussions. Expensive lesson.

In the early 1980s I'd gone to stay with Marsha in California. I was broke at the time. It was while I was struggling as a single mum. I felt a pull from the place. I remember thinking, 'This is what I want. I'm going to come and live here.'

I returned to England with two fabulous pink party dresses with layers of pink net petticoats; one for Phoebe and one for Chloe. They were an enormous hit. Since then we've always said that living in California is 'living in the pink'. It's bubble gum. It's candy floss. Now I live in a pink cottage in Malibu.

I brought the dresses home as symbols of what I was going to give them someday, somehow. I'd no idea how, though. And then I dropped it. It was like putting a message in a box, or a wish or a prayer, and then burying it.

The Colbys

In the television series *The Colbys* my character was married to Charlton Heston's, had Barbara Stanwyck for a sister-in-law and a sister played by Katharine Ross.

First day on the set I wasn't nervous until I thought, 'That's Barbara Stanwyck and *this* is Hollywood.' Later that day I had a scene with Linda Evans. I'm completely deaf in my right ear. The shot had been blocked with Linda standing on my right. I couldn't hear my cue. I swapped sides. Linda was very gracious about it. I had to take a glass of champagne from a tray a waiter was carrying with my left hand. I was really nervous. My hand was trembling so I thought it seemed wiser to take the glass with my right. I had to re-orchestrate the whole scene. I thought, 'Don't start justifying this, Stephanie, just do what you have to do to survive, and be your best.'

California

California came as an amazing gift. England felt arid. It was monochrome. It had become devoid of all colour. It was time to move. I knew how the pioneers must have felt.

Phoebe and Chloe came over and spent the rest of the summer holidays with me. They were already in a sweet little boarding school near my parents. It was like St Trinian's with horses. They loved it. They'd started going there when I was doing *Connie*. We'd tried nannies but it hadn't worked. I'd sold the big house in West Hampstead and down-sized to more practical accommodation. I had no idea what was around the corner. No idea that I was putting everything in place so California could happen. When it came to meet me, there was nothing in my way.

I'd been blacklisted from making movies and now the people in power were different and I'd come back via television. I knew how to do publicity now. I'd learned, and anything I didn't know I was going to ask. I have no problem with asking now. I am perfectly happy to say, 'I don't understand, will you tell me?' and that's a very important thing for all of us to be able to do. It's fine not to know; it's not fine not to ask, and it's not fine not to remember once you've been told. We're too proud to ask, so we often don't.

In California my whole world turned Technicolor. I'd always end up going to the beach. I couldn't actually believe that I could live under blue sunny skies by the sea and go to work and earn a fortune. It was amazing. All the time I was feeling 'my cup runneth over' – for the children, too. I was walking up hills, seeing the most beautiful views. The atmosphere was so relaxed, so casual. One day I'd just come back from the studio, make-up on, hair perfect. I was in the supermarket. The girl on the till gave me a pitying look.

'Oh dear, been in town?' she asked. It wasn't – 'Oh, you look nice.' No, it was: 'Been in town? – Poor you.' That's Malibu.

People used to say, 'How can you live in America?' and I'd say, 'Well, I'm only ten years ahead of what's happening in England.' It caught up eventually. California living was new and thrilling. Now, in the UK, gyms abound. People know about healthy living and right eating, and there's a big network of alternative healing available. Forgive me for being so thrilled with being in America 25 years ago, but England was a lot different then from how it is now. We'd had the miners' strike and there was a woman in Number 10 who seemed to me to be a man in drag, God bless her.

Los Angeles was fabulous. I was amused: I'm supposed to be leading the second half of my life totally spiritually and here I am on a more commercial path than I ever thought I'd be. Sorry, God, I don't think I'm quite doing what was intended.

I was settling in but the kids weren't with me. I was really missing them but I felt the boarding school routine would give them stability. And then I realized I was missing something else. When you're at the centre of it all, suddenly on the front cover of *TV Guide*, and getting invitations from everybody, it's all pretty heady stuff. But these are fair-weather friends; they're not long term – treating you as if they've known you for a long time but they've only known you for a week and they don't know you anyway, they only know Sable Colby. It was hard to be *really* seen. It was hard to have a centre.

My rather loose way of prayer suddenly didn't have foundation enough. I needed to find a church and start going to it. I was already rather Buddhist in leaning, so I joined a Nichiren Daishonin temple and got my Gohonzon. Barbara Ronci, my hairdresser, had introduced me to this. I'd told her that I felt I was being pushed into a gilded cage and she'd suggested I go and chant with her. I was getting in and out of limos, being pampered and treated in the most extraordinary way, but I needed to keep my feet on the ground and keep in contact with the higher power. I really needed that. It's still very important to me.

Nichiren Daishonin served me for a while but I started to question the materialistic motivation of many of the temple's members. I'd embraced Catholicism and I knew I loved Buddhism, but I couldn't fully commit. It was rather depressing. That's when I went to Ron Scolastico and was told that my inability to settle was bound up with what had happened in a past life.

What the psychics had told me and then landing up in Hollywood all seemed rather contradictory, until I realized that Southern California is the home of the spiritual seeker. There, the openness to spiritual enquiry is massive.

After my experience with hospitals and surgery I was never going to be trusting of traditional medicine again, and Southern California has every alternative therapy treatment and approach lined up and waiting. I was looking for a doctor and was advised to see a Dr Wagner in Bonsall Canyon, Malibu. Dr Wagner practises applied kinesiology. He muscle-tested me for homoeopathic medicines. A whole new way of looking at things began to open up.

Ava

My first real contact with Hollywood was through Ava Gardner. I co-starred with her and Ian McShane in the film *Tam Lin* in 1969, a couple of years after leaving RADA. We had taken over the Peebles Hydro in Scotland. The place was crawling with crew, equipment and a cast that included Cyril Cusack, who was playing my father, Cyril's real-life daughter – Sinead Cusack – Joanna Lumley, Richard Wattis and our director, Roddy McDowall. All we lacked was our star.

Ava arrived chauffeured like royalty, with her corgis, a gramophone player and a box of Frank Sinatra records. He'd been her third and last husband and, though divorced, their love never died. I stayed in my room when she arrived. I thought she'd have far more important people to meet. I was young and unknown. She was a seasoned star, a Hollywood legend. It was a mistake – she felt snubbed. She'd wanted to meet her young co-star. I was still learning. We made up, though, and became friends. She was a lovely person to work with; she mentored me and I was hungry to learn from her. She'd get me to stand on a box during scenes in which we had dialogue. I asked her why. 'The lights are far kinder to the older face when it's looking up rather than down: bags under the eyes – gone.' She knew all the tricks.

I remembered this trick when on the set of *Dynasty* one day, when we were doing close-ups. Just as we were about to go for a take, Joan Collins, in full regalia as her character Alexis Carrington, kicked her shoes off.

'Oh my feet, they're so sore,' she said, with a huge sigh.

Without her heels my eye line was going to be considerably lower.

'Oh gosh,' I said, 'I *so* know what you mean.' I looked at her discarded shoes and measured up the heel in my mind. 'Could we have a four-and-a-half-inch pancake – techie-speak for what's essentially a box – for Miss Collins, please?' I asked the chippies.

Ava Gardner was of course a great beauty. In her heyday, during the late 1940s and throughout the 1950s, she'd been *the* Hollywood *femme fatale*. She was 46 when we worked together, and losing confidence in her looks – but I saw a flash of the legendary beauty that had so entranced audiences. In a fit of pique she'd thrown three Mason and Pearson hairbrushes at her hairdresser, Sydney Guilaroff, a star in his own right. Her eyes turned a piercing green, her forehead rose and her cheekbones became accentuated. Her inner Contessa literally smouldered with presence. If I was her director I'd keep her angry all the time, I thought.

Ava taught me many things and was wonderful company. Her laughter was catching, a deep throaty chortle. I've seen her dance on tables and slam doors. A mass of contradictions, she was a firm believer in marriage even though she'd made such a foul mess of hers. A fabulous woman.

Marlon

My second contact with Hollywood happened the next year. I co-starred with Marlon Brando in *The Nightcomers*. I'd already worked with the film's director, Michael Winner, on his film *The Games*. I knew how Michael worked and Michael knew how I worked. Marlon's reputation was that he was unique and difficult. Michael thought he would have his hands full. He needed Marlon's co-star to be reliable and easy to direct – a grunt. That was me.

'What's the part?' I asked when we met to discuss the film.

'Well, my dear,' he barked, 'it's a good role but what I will tell you now is that it entails a degree of freedom of clothes.'

I wanted to meet Marlon before working with him so that if he wanted me to be fired it would be done before we got to the set. Michael arranged an evening at his house. He also invited John Trevelyan, the Secretary of the British Board of Film Censors. It was political. John Trevelyan took a hard line when it came to on-screen nudity. During the course of the evening the conversation turned to Zen Buddhism. I joined in and John Trevelyan cut me off while I was speaking. I felt embarrassed and humiliated. Sitting next to me, Marlon put his hand on mine as a sign of solidarity, support and reassurance. It was a warm and generous gesture. We became great friends, and he was fascinating to work with.

Marlon was a special, gifted and very talented man – a true star in every sense of the word. His fame and physical beauty

Drawing Marlon doodled on the back of my script for me

meant nothing to him. Far more important were his sense of personal integrity and his commitment to the various causes he supported throughout his life. His gestures of solidarity and support came to anyone he felt was being unfairly treated.

The Nightcomers was far from the best movie ever made, but I'm incredibly grateful for having been able to work on it. It gave me the gift of my friendship with Marlon, and the honour of co-starring alongside the actor named as the fourth greatest male star of all time by the American Film Institute.

Marlon had had his fair share of fellow actors playing games with him. Over the years, he'd been so mucked around while doing reverse shots, by actors taking his focus away from the camera, that he preferred to do his close-ups to a white piece of tape on the camera. He explained that I needn't be there when he did his close-ups, but I told him I'd rather be.

'That's very sweet of you,' he said, 'but you don't have to be.'

'Of course I do,' I replied, 'because I want you there for me.'

I was too young to understand that people didn't talk to Brando like that, telling him that he had to be there for my reverses. I was too young to understand how you did or didn't talk to a great star. I'm sure that's why we became friends: I was honest with him.

Sharing life's ups and downs, usually by phone, we were in touch right up until he died. One time he confided in me that he felt he'd been a bad parent and couldn't understand why, since he loved his children so much.

'You're that man in the cap riding his motorbike on the front of millions of T-shirts, Marlon. How many living stars are on a T-shirt? You're an icon. That's a hard thing for any child to have to deal with.'

Charlton Heston

Working with Chuck was a delight. He really was called Chuck. He phoned me when he was diagnosed with Alzheimer's: 'I wanted to tell you, my dear, before I forget, that I love you.' I love that man very much.

I only saw Chuck dry up on his lines once. It was during a scene when we were being nasty to each other. I said something typically Sable, and hurtfully barbed, to him and he turned to shout at me. All of a sudden, he just dried. I asked him if he was OK and what the matter was.

'I just caught your children's eyes,' he said, softly. 'They looked so shocked.' Phoebe and Chloe were on the set, witnessing our fight. Chuck had noticed the discomfort in their eyes and felt responsible. He'd had to stop – dear man.

We were at a Christmas party one year, up at Chuck and his wife Lydia's house. I didn't know where Phoebe was and I was worried. She was only nine and there were a lot of people there. Suddenly I spotted her. I asked her where she'd been. 'Oh, I was with him,' she said, pointing to Chuck. 'He was showing me the stick that turns into a snake.' I turned to him. 'You're the only man who could show a child a stick that turns into a snake and I wouldn't call the police.' He'd been showing her Moses' staff – or, rather, the prop he'd used when he played Moses in the epic *Ten Commandments*.

Tony Robbins

I came across Tony Robbins at 5 o'clock one morning while I was stretching before going to work and he was leering out of the TV with his huge white-toothed smile. He was advertising a set of self-help cassette tapes and saying, 'If you don't make more money than these tapes cost in the first two weeks of doing them, you can ask for your money back.' I thought, 'OK, you're on,' and I ordered them.

They were wonderful. They came into my life at exactly the right time. I'd listen to them while I was driving. One was about procrastination, another was about scarcity, and another was about the availability of multiple choices, and the option we always have to see things differently. Tony's tapes helped me to save money and to make more money, just like he'd promised.

I'd landed a role in *Sea Quest*, for Steven Spielberg. I was going to be playing a marine biologist and had to learn as much as I could on the subject. There's no better place to do that than the Scripps Institution of Oceanography in San Diego. I was wondering how I was going to be able to get in there. I thought 'Tony Robbins' – approach it differently. I realized that what I had to do was phone Spielberg's office and ask them to set up a meeting for me with a marine biologist. I thought I had to do it on my own, but it was perfectly OK to ask. They were delighted. They arranged the most extraordinary set-up for me. They picked me up, took me to the research institute, gave me just what I needed and saved me an enormous amount of money. The visit taught me a great deal and I found the woman I based my character on. Unfortunately, the day before we started shooting I was made the ship's doctor, too. One evening is rather a short time to squeeze four years of med school into. Ah, well, you win some, you lose some!

Tony Robbins also stopped me from being such a terrible procrastinator. He enabled me to look at things differently and to organize myself in such a way that my list of problems was no longer so long and daunting. He showed me that I could live with far less worry and fear.

Coming to California was a huge opportunity: I was being given the chance to change. Fear was telling me not to change. I didn't know if the negative patterns had become too ingrained. I didn't know if I was dug in too deep. I didn't know if that British tendency towards self-effacement was so well-rooted I'd be unable to learn afresh. The thing is, if you think you can't, you won't be able to. Show a child something and they have no limitations on the possibilities that they could achieve. I started to think, 'Baby, change if you can.' Tony Robbins helped me see that I could.

Anthony Perkins

As soon as Anthony Perkins and I met, we started laughing. So many of the best of my friendships have started with a similar sense of humour. We were in Paris filming *Napoleon and Josephine: A Love Story*. Tony missed his family and I missed mine. He was working his way through *A Course in Miracles*. Every day we'd read some passages. It's an enormous tome but its wisdom boils down to the truth that everything we do in our lives is driven by either love or fear.

There are some very good restaurants in Paris, and we slowly worked our way through most of them and spent a lot of time fancying the same waiters. He was a bad boy, and I loved him.

We'd meet up and go to the Tutankhamun exhibition; we went to the Louvre; we went everywhere in Paris where there was anything to be seen.

Tony said, 'If you're going to be a thin actor, don't just be a thin actor, be the thinnest actor in the world. What are we going to eat, Stephanie?' I became the fattest actress in the world because he didn't do any eating, he'd just choose what *I* was going to eat. He was very controlling but I got him.

I asked him if he loved his wife – the glorious Berry Berenson. 'Yes!' he said.

I asked him 'How much?'

'Totally,' he replied.

'No, I mean how much do you love her? Do you love her your *per diem*?' A *per diem* is what you get given to live on when you're on a job away from home. Like me, Tony was able to live on much less than what we were given.

'That's a bit rich,' he said.

'OK, do you love her 10 per cent? Do you love her a tithe of your *per diem*?'

'Of course,' he said.

'Give it to me, then,' I ordered.

'What?' he shot back.

'Give it to me – 10 per cent of two months' money.' We went to Boucheron or Cartier, I can't remember which, and bought her a wonderful piece, a bracelet. She told me later it was the only piece of jewellery he had ever given her. What fun.

We were having a Parisian adventure while also adventuring spiritually. Tony was completely caught up by *A Course in Miracles*, and convinced me, too, of the idea that there is only love or fear. Every time I find myself up against a brick wall, thinking, 'I don't think so,' I ask myself: Is this a decision I'm making because I'm frightened, or am I being loving? It's really quite profound, and it's really quite difficult, but it's a good question to ask. Is this decision good for you and good for everybody else – in your highest good, and therefore in the highest good of everybody else? Or is it motivated by fear?

Tony Perkins was also the first person to make me question my subconscious. He helped me recognize those terribly damaging patterns I'd learned, and to separate these from what was true intuition. If someone shows you something orange and you say, 'Oh no, I hate orange,' chances are you hate orange because there's some story in your past that's led to you having a bad experience with orange. If you can manage to stop yourself, and question those immediate thoughts, you can start to look behind them and see what's really going on.

We've all got horrid bits in our subconscious – ideas and thoughts about ourselves that aren't true. We tell ourselves all sorts of things that are quite simply, false: 'you're not good enough, you can't do that, you're not worthy of that.' Tony would question me the whole time. He wasn't always right, though. Sometimes he'd make me roar with laughter.

'You're looking at people, Stephanie,' he'd say.

'Sure I am,' I'd reply. 'I love people-watching.'

'No, you're the star – they stare at you, you just look straight ahead.'

This was a man who used to wear shoulder pads in his T-shirts because he was *so* skinny. He'd decided to be the skinniest actor there ever was and he was going for it. I loved him. On my *This Is Your Life* he made a very flattering speech that made me blush. I didn't watch the programme until two years later. I was in Bristol staying with my friends Sue and Adrian, and they had it on video. At 8:30 one morning I thought I'd watch it. I saw it, then turned on the radio. I caught the news that Tony Perkins had died. He'd just waved me goodbye.

Hollywood Royalty

Through my darling 90-year-old friend Richard Gully, I had the privilege of meeting and dining with many of the old guard of Hollywood stars. It was an absolute delight.

With Richard Gully at my 46th birthday party

Every Wednesday evening he would have a dinner arranged at the best table at Le Dome on Sunset Plaza. He would invite people he'd worked with and enjoyed over his many years as a Hollywood publicist, and people visiting from Europe. There would be a Duke next to Mitzi Gaynor next to Howard Keel next to Esther Williams, and so on.

Richard always insisted on driving himself to these dinners in a car that was as old and dignified as he was, a Bentley I think it was, but the steering wheel was extremely loose and frankly I'm amazed we always arrived safely.

On one of my birthdays Burt Bacharach sang 'Happy Birthday' to me. On another occasion Howard Keel serenaded me with 'Oh, What a Beautiful Morning' from *Oklahoma!*

One of the great sillinesses, though, was with Cyd Charisse and Tony Martin. I'd had dinner with them lots of times. I was with my younger daughter Chloe at the premier of Matthew Bourne's *Cinderella* in Los Angeles, this would have been 1997, and Cyd and Tony were sitting in front of us. I introduced Chloe, saying, 'Chloe, this is Cyd Charisse and Tony Martin.' 'Nice to meet you, Sid,' Chloe said, leaning over to Tony Martin. Cyd Charisse's face was a picture. I told Chloe I didn't think we'd be going to the after party. We didn't.

Then there were the women writers.

Danielle Steel, what a fabulous woman. She writes a book and she buys a piece of jewellery. She has better jewellery than anyone else I've ever known. I thoroughly enjoyed being in the film version of her book *Secrets* and getting to know her a bit.

I was also in Barbara Taylor-Bradford's *To Be the Best* with Anthony Hopkins, Lindsay Wagner and Chris Cazenove; we met on a lawn in Washington, D.C. at a lunch for the Queen and Prince Philip. I was also in Jackie Collins' *Lucky Chances*. When we met, Jackie said, 'I don't know if I should be talking to you.' I'd played a writer called Vicki Sprantz in *Troop Beverly Hills*. It was obvious I'd based her on Jackie – I wore every sort of animal print I could. But Esther Shapiro, who created *Dynasty* and *The Colbys*, was the woman who made the biggest impression on me. When Esther spoke, I listened and did just what she advised. She speaks very softly and is very wise.

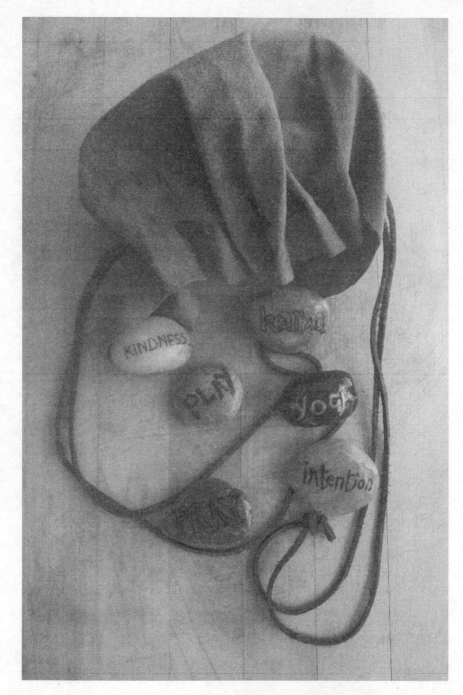

My toolbag of shiny stones

Chapter Ten

Big Words in a
Little Toolbag

Wherever I go in the world I'll visit a beautiful cathedral or church, temple or mosque. I pray every day, but I don't attend services on a regular basis. I haven't found a resting place; I'm still a wandering gypsy.

I don't have one spiritual home, but I do have a toolbag. I imagine it like a medieval suede bag slung over my shoulder, with all the shiny stones from those amazing experiences I've had. Coming to live in California, meeting people who understand my jackdaw nature and the point of the message I was given by the three psychics, has meant I've been in the perfect place to collect more shiny stones and learn how to use them. It's also a place where people I've met haven't thought that the things I've experienced in the past are implausible.

Those stones have become a compass for my life, and the tools I use to help me. I've realized that things I once thought were terribly serious, and rather difficult to understand, are actually not like that at all, and that I can use them in very practical ways.

161

Therapy

I wanted to go to the Café Malibu and didn't fancy going by myself, so I phoned this guy I'd dated a few times. I hadn't seen him for a couple of months, but on a whim I decided to call him. He said he was tired but would meet me there. When he walked in I couldn't believe it. He looked *so* alive. Whatever he's on, I thought, I want it. I asked him what had happened and he told me he'd just done The Forum. I felt I needed a jolt so I did it, too. I found it really useful. It's a personal development programme that helps you get behind the scams you set up when you're a child, and that have been covertly governing your life ever since. It helped me start living more honestly with myself and others.

The guy was Colin. Since that time, he and I have shared a path and a friendship. We're the first to admit that it's a work in progress, and that every day we have struggles with ourselves. I can have a tendency to be terribly controlling and Colin to be very judgemental. We call each other 'Judgement' and 'Control'.

Colin started dating my friend Lindsay Wagner. She and I had met and become friends while we were filming *To Be the Best* with Anthony Hopkins in Hong Kong. Colin thought she was wonderful, which she is, but he couldn't stop going on and on about her and I said something mean. Colin glared at me. 'You'll only be forgiven for that remark if you spend one thousand dollars on yourself – not on your children – and do ten sessions with Margie Paul.'

Margie Paul has developed a very simple and practical approach to emotional health – it's called Inner Bonding. It's a therapeutic process of personal development, but with a strong

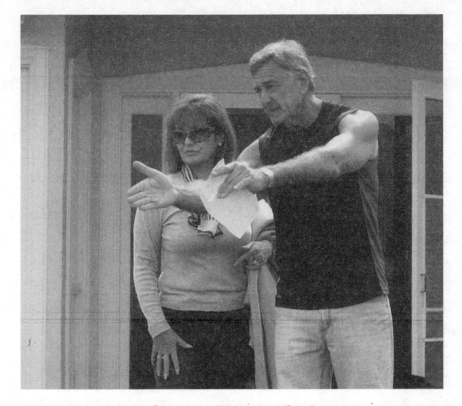

Colin and me – 'Judgement' and 'Control'

leaning towards the spiritual. It acknowledges that we've all been wounded in our lives in one way or another and need to heal, but it emphasizes that we're responsible for our own healing. It also encourages people to connect with God, or spirit, or however you define the higher power, and to start living as a loving adult rather than a wounded child. I have to have practical solutions, and Inner Bonding provides one. Every time I've been like a little Tonka truck and driven myself right into a wall and got stuck, Inner Bonding has helped me go into reverse, back up then carry on my way.

The Daily Routine

For Muslims, the 'call to prayer' really is a call to prayer, five times a day. I find that most inspiring. I have spiritual purpose; I just don't have spiritual form. I've stopped worrying about it and just get on with my own routine.

We all have our habits and routines, like teeth-cleaning and hair-brushing. I've developed a few spiritual routines. I start my day with a quick prayer – a moment of gratitude in silence. I invent a new prayer each day, so that it doesn't become a mindless habit. It doesn't need to be any more elaborate than 'Thank you for this wonderful day, so full of opportunity, that I'm now beginning.'

Mentally I go through the list of what I've planned to do that day, checking off the 'to do' list I made the night before. I may forget my list during the day but the important things will get done without me having to think about them. I like to start each day with optimism. When we were rehearsing *Master Class*, Jonathan Church, the director, commented, 'It's amazing, Stephanie, but every day, never mind how bad yesterday was, you walk into rehearsals with such positive energy.' I said, 'Thank you, Jonathan,' and I thought, 'Thank you, God.'

Without really thinking about it, and certainly not actively going in search of it, what the three psychics told me has definitely come to be. When I was softened by motherhood, after Phoebe was born, I couldn't possibly have refuted God. Exploring what that means for me personally has become an important part of my life.

Karma

When life doesn't seem to make sense, and God is a step too far, I never fall lower than karma. That's the bottom line of truth for me and it's really simple. If something's not plain and simple and down to earth, what use is it to us mere mortals?

According to karma, what you do is what you are. Give a child too much sugar and you could get a raging tantrum. You might say, 'That's not karma, that's chemicals.' I think karma can involve chemicals. Karma is action and result, it's cause and effect; they're the same thing. Without a spiritual practice I don't feel complete and whole. If I don't do any exercise, my muscles wither, my metabolism goes out of kilter and I feel out of sorts. This is cause and effect, action and result; it's karma. Someone can steal and get away with it, but they're still a thief. It makes so much sense. I love it. It's a simple and practical concept that enables me to accept responsibility for who I am at any moment.

I believe that if we ignore karma and don't do the work we're here to do this time round, we're going to meet the same lessons again and again until the work's been done. We come into life with a 'to-do' list; it's not written down, but it's there. Homework does not get excused.

Mindfulness

The days rush by so fast. I try to take time to meditate and stay calm and see the beauty in any situation. Meditation is sometimes hard. If I'm in a really public place I just breathe in on one word, and breathe out on another. I make up a simple mantra that's easy to repeat; two words, like 'love' on the in-breath and 'being' as I exhale. As I go round and round with them, they become 'being, love' as well as 'love, being'. I don't make it any more complicated than that. There's no need to do more than have a straight spine and concentrate on breathing. You'd look pretty silly trying to do full Lotus Position on a crowded train. Meditation's purpose is to clear the mind and become present. It lowers my blood pressure and makes me calm. In the evening, there are always questions I'll have about my day. I'll often use the Bible, the runes, animal medicine cards or sayings from the Dalai Lama, to reflect on the day and find answers to the questions that have come up. I use these divinatory tools as a way of contacting my innermost feelings.

I always keep a little book of positive wisdom tucked in a pocket to take out and find a good phrase in, throughout the day. It's uplifting.

In my diary I have written: Have a GREAT Day!

G – Give

R – Relate to others

E – Exercise

A – Attend to the world around

T – Try something new

I love this little list; I carry it with me wherever I go. My boyfriend Bernie gave it to me; it's from The Happiness Institute.

Dr David Hawkins, the author of *Power vs Force*, among other books, has been developing theories about human consciousness for the last 50 years. All of them have practical applications. Dr Hawkins highlights the relationship between emotions and vibrational frequencies. His 'Map of Consciousness' lays out a spectrum of emotional states, each of which he has calibrated with a corresponding frequency. They range from low – for example, shame calibrates at 20, guilt at 30 and fear at 100 – to the highest states – where enlightenment calibrates from 700 to 1,000, and unconditional love and a dog's wagging tail calibrate at 540. A moment of joy, by the way, is also 540. I try to keep my calibration level as high as possible. I seldom get over 250, which is neutrality, but I'm happy if I get to 310, which is willingness.

Trying to maintain as high a calibration level as possible requires remaining mindful of what is happening in the present and what feelings are being experienced from moment to moment. It might sound obvious and simple, but it isn't. It's hard to shift from having a defensive and fearful attitude to having a willingness to learn and an attitude of openness and loving. Using Dr Hawkins' tables and charts makes the process easier. It's a bit like a Weight Watchers point system for the emotions, rather than the calories.

Divination

I love the runes. They're an Old Norse system of divination. I love animal medicine cards, too. Whether it's the runes, animal cards, the I Ching or the stars, you're accessing your subconscious. They're all methods of divination. Each applies a set of variables, representing your world, against a variety of meanings. Each has its own structure and set of codified meanings. They're like combination locks to the vault of the subconscious. I always see my readings as positive, even if they're warning me of something.

Intuition

When Phoebe was a baby she always used to have a morning nap in the basement. One day, for some reason I decided not to put her down there. There was a flash flood and the basement turned into a lake. The house's wiring came from the fuse box in the basement. If Phoebe had been sleeping there that morning, she would have been electrocuted.

Another time I was in Selfridges, rushing around – however fast a person can move through their life. I suddenly thought, 'I've got to go to Chester Street.' It was where my friend Christina lived, but not the same house where the fire had happened in 1996. I didn't know why, I just knew I had to go there, so I went. When I got there her son Nicky was sitting on the wall looking very miserable. 'I knew you'd come,' he said. He'd put a call out for me; a mental call. He knew that I'd come, and I did. He had total faith, total trust. What was that? Telepathy? My mother could heal telepathically. Is that some kind of fine-tuning? I don't know, but if a mother's love was great enough I think she could find her baby in a blizzard.

Determination

When I want something, I reach for it and take practical steps. I've always been like that. When I was at RADA my scholarship wasn't covering my outgoings. I wrote to Barnet Borough Council:

Dear Sirs

I would like to take this opportunity to thank you from the bottom of my heart for the bursary you have very kindly awarded me that is enabling me to study at the Royal Academy of Dramatic Art. I cannot emphasise enough how extremely grateful I am for your generosity.

As you know I have every intention of being a very famous actress one day but I find that I am not able to keep myself in tights, and as I am sure you will understand I just won't wear laddered stockings. I am going to be such a good representative of the grant you have kindly given me that if you could possibly find it in yourselves to give me an extra pound a week in order for me to look respectable then I would be incredibly grateful.

Yours faithfully

They may have laughed when they read it, but they gave me that extra pound.

It was this determination to do something about my situation that got me off the floor after I became an emotional wreck and was struggling as a single parent.

Getting Out of My Own Way

This is the way I do it: I let go and let God and get out of my own way. But I can't let go if I haven't done the work. I can't just let go and expect God to do the work.

When I let go of my ego, I let go of the outcome. If I've already made up my mind about what I want the outcome to be, I've already limited the possibilities.

I like this little Zen story:

A farmer's son was riding his horse when he fell off and broke his leg. His father said, 'This is a tragedy; my son's an invalid.' The Zen monk said, 'We'll see.' Later all the young men were called up to fight in the war. The boy couldn't go because he'd broken his leg. The father said, 'This is terrible; my son can't join the young men and fight for his country.' 'We'll see,' said the Zen monk. None of the young men came home.

When I was wallowing in self-pity, thinking the life I'd known had come to an end, I was getting in my own way. As soon as I let go and let God, my life began to change.

Self-responsibility

I'll eat a blueberry muffin if I really want to, but the chances are I'll start the day with protein because it'll give me a longer supply of fuel. I'm a coffee addict. A Japanese healer told me, 'One cup is medicine, two is poison.' If I can only have one cup I make sure it's the best so I can really enjoy it. And if I have more than one, I'm aware that I'm poisoning myself.

I walk somewhere pretty, jog somewhere pleasant. I make it a spiritual experience. It doesn't have to be in hills, woods or by the sea. There is always the park or the pavement.

Separate your woes into different piles. It makes them so much easier to cope with. Twenty problems piled on top of each other are impossible to deal with.

Phone a Friend

I was rushing back to England to say goodbye to my mother. I was going to her funeral and memorial service. I had a complete meltdown over packing my suitcase. I was crying and making the whole situation more awful than it already was. I just couldn't do it. And then, like in *Who Wants to Be a Millionaire*, I thought, 'Phone a friend!' I called Philip and Steve, two of my best friends. They live in Houston now but were still living in Los Angeles then. Philip's a minister but when I met him he was a film producer. We laughed from the second we met. Steve is one of the cleverest people I know. They both make me roar with laughter. They used to be Catholic but now they're Presbyterians. They're also on a spiritual search, and they're great searching companions. They're a fabulous couple and we've seen each other through a lot. I phoned them and told them what was happening. They came round, we talked it through and, before I knew it, my suitcase was packed. Death is hard to face alone.

You are allowed to ask for help, but be specific. We shouldn't make the whole of ourselves somebody else's responsibility, but it is OK to phone a friend with a particular problem. It's a totally legitimate thing to do. Taking responsibility doesn't mean being an island.

Thoughtfulness

Marlon Brando was very keen on mouthwash. 'Even though the script might say two people are attracted to each other, you can't force it in real life but the least you can do is make yourself presentable,' he said once. *The* method actor of all time still had the consideration to know that mouthwash is a good idea if you're in close contact with other actors.

Playfulness and Creativity

Playing is an attitude. I play when I'm cooking, which makes my meals pretty hit or miss. Children play when they're having a bath. Daydreaming is playing. Painting, sewing, writing, mending: endless playing. Do the things the world considers to be important, but make sure you feed your soul by playing. Release yourself from all standards: they hold us back. Most of them have been inflicted on us and they stop us from playing. I love to paint. If you saw my paintings you might well think I've no talent for it. But that's not the point. It's a question of just doing it and playing with my imagination.

I feel I've got two bank accounts: one for money and one for spirit. My spiritual bank account has to be full; otherwise my light turns off, like Tinkerbell. Most of the theatre jobs I've done can't be justified by the money they paid. Why would I do them? I do some jobs to fill my spiritual bank account, nourish my spirit and feed me creatively. Others pay the bills. Sometimes it's possible to fill both at the same time, and usually every job has its moments. Those moments of joy when you're working hard are a real gift. Joy isn't something you can demand or expect. It's a gift.

I remember sitting in the kitchen of our house in West Hampstead. The children were in bed. It was winter and cold. I was faced with a pile of bills and two scripts for two jobs I was being offered. One was for a play that I really wanted to do, and one was for a film that I really wasn't interested in. At that point in my life I didn't have the luxury to choose. The bills needed to be paid. The film was a low-budget sci-fi horror called *Inseminoid*. It might have been a bad film, but it kept food on our table and was actually a lot of fun to do. Judy Geeson and I laughed and played our way through the whole production. It was at a time in my life when I badly needed to laugh and play again. Taking on that job was absolutely the right choice.

I hear people talk disapprovingly about the Lottery. If one pound can stimulate that amount of imagining, let everybody put their pound in on a Saturday night and dream about how much munificence they'd bring to the planet. I believe in the Lottery if only for the dreaming. It's not even the dream of money; it's the dream of what you could do. That's playing.

My friend Bitten Knudsen was one of my greatest playing partners. Her laugh will stay with me for ever. She was so beautiful – blonde perfection itself. Among other things, she modelled for *Vogue* and all the big fashion magazines. We were both Pisces and we both needed the ocean. We called ourselves the sea slugs. Bitten also needed the city; she'd take off for New York so she could hit hard pavement. We once went to a Matisse exhibition then afterwards spent days and days painting in the Matisse style. Bitten was completely wild, and fearless. I've always enjoyed my fearless friends; you can play so hard with them. Bitten took playing a bit too far, though, and died far too young.

With Bitten in New York

I also play spiritually; and why not? I did some soul retrieval work with a shaman. There's nothing kooky about shamanism. It's probably the oldest form of medicine and healing on the planet, and has been part of human activity, in one form or other, on every continent – it still is. I visited a lady called Amanda, up in a leafy part of Topanga Canyon, who uses shamanism as a tool for healing, guidance and personal development. If you've had an enormous trauma, part of your soul goes to live somewhere else. Soul-retrieval involves finding where that is and getting it back. I don't quite know why my ex-husband should have taken my feet, but that's what seemed to have happened. Maybe he had, because he always used to tease me about the way my toes turned in. I tend to stand with my feet in a turned out position, but my toes naturally turn in. He'd taken my feet; my joyful dancing feet. I got them back in such a vivid way. How could it be that I was on the back of a panther, leaping across rivers and up trees; where did that come from?

It's a bit like when you're dreaming and you wake up and think, 'Oh dear, being awake doesn't feel nearly as real as that did.' I was entranced by the experience; I was in trance. It was very powerful.

Shamanic journeying was another thing I did with Amanda. That also involved going into a trance, then going on an image-streaming journey into the Earth. It started no more strangely than a doctor's appointment. Amanda asked me to lie down on a blanket on the floor and close my eyes. A drum began a very steady beat, and then Amanda told me I had to enter the Earth and go to the lower world where I would meet my spirit guides. 'How do I get into the Earth?' I asked. 'Think of a place where you can see the ground open,' she replied. 'Can I make myself tiny?' 'Yes,' I was told. I thought of the little stream that came out of the ground, near the old house on Dartmoor. I imagined myself as really tiny and slipped into the Earth alongside the stream. It was all taking place as visualization but was becoming completely real. I saw a little animal trotting along. It turned to face me, but continued to trot, and began to lead the way. It was a fox. Ever since, the fox has been a very important animal for me – one of my animal spirit guides.

This little foxy darling led me from one adventure to another until, finally, we went up a hill where a Native American was sorting 12 charred sticks from a small fire. He turned to me. 'Just because you have facility, doesn't mean you can be facile,' he said. I was jolted out of my trance and that was the end of the journey.

I've also been to a sweat lodge. That didn't really do it for me. I thought it was probably one of the most disgusting, smelly things I've ever done. I couldn't understand why you'd want to use steaming hot stones when you can just go into a perfectly nice electrically-heated sauna and do the same thing. It was a bit too old fashioned. I know it's different and there's chanting, but I didn't get it. I was simply faint with the heat. I did get to be in

Urban fox, Brighton shopping arcade

another space, but it was called dehydration. Spiritual bungee jumping – without a doubt.

Attitude

Sometimes I find myself feeling discontented; I forget that, really, I have more than enough. I really don't need any more. Sometimes I get caught in the thought that I live in a universe that's limited by scarcity. Then I notice there's little gratitude for what I *do* have. Whenever I notice that I'm feeling envious or insecure, I try to think about what I have that I am grateful for. It's the most practical thing I can do and it stops me from looking sideways. When I'm doing that, I'm looking at people as competition. There's only one person I have to deal with, really, and that's myself. If I find myself feeling envious, I really give myself a good talking to. Be pleased for other people's achievements – they're proof it can be done.

If you can't change the circumstances, change your attitude.

Procrastination

Procrastination is the enemy of free time. Do what needs to be done now. I often think I'll get round to whatever it is eventually, but at the moment I don't have the time. The fact is, I don't want to do it. We'll do anything to avoid doing things that are painful, but if they're going to come around anyway, it's best to do them before they become more painful, like paying that parking ticket.

I used to put off paying parking tickets until they'd gone beyond the fine and passed through the court. I got to know the bailiff so well we were on first-name terms. 'Hello, is that Stephanie again?' the receptionist used to say whenever I called their office.

I used to use smoking as a tool for procrastination. I'd put off doing things until I'd had a cigarette. I smoked for many years until I saw a friend at a dinner party. She looked so good, I asked her what she'd done. She'd given up smoking. I gave up smoking on the day George W. Bush was re-elected. I couldn't do anything about the world, but I could change myself. I haven't smoked since.

Think Ahead and Eat That Chocolate

When I was young and going out I kept a £5 note sewn into the lining of my jacket – just in case. Today it would probably need to be a £50 note. I didn't know if I was going to find myself in a sticky situation. That £5 note would have got me out of it: away from the rough crowd. It could have got me a train or a taxi. I wouldn't have to get into a stranger's car in order to get a lift home. It was my emergency money. The clubs in Soho in the early Sixties had the best music, but it was a part of London from which you needed to be ready to make a quick getaway.

It's the practicalities in life I like to remember. I know the lines for the audition, but do I know where the audition is being held? Do I know what time I have to be there, and have I ironed my skirt?

If you need some retail therapy, sew a £50 note into the hem of your jacket and think of it as money you've spent on your own protection. Invest in looking after yourself. If there's nothing you want more right now than a bar of chocolate – drink a pint of water to make sure that your stomach is full. Eat some greens and some protein. You still really want that chocolate? Go and buy it. Eat one square and give the rest away. You've got what you needed.

Be conscious of what you're doing from moment to moment. This is the essence of practical consciousness.

With any addictive behaviour, there's always way more going on. When I realized that, I started thinking about getting some really practical therapy. I wasn't interested in going to see some therapist who was going to nod wisely, listen and say, 'I'll see you the same time next week.' I might as well just talk to a friend on the telephone. I see no point in that. For me, Inner Bonding is about as good as it gets, and I fell into that by serendipity and being bitchy.

Intention

This is another of the big words. If it's your intention to learn, you will. If it's your intention to succeed, you'd better know what you're going to succeed in first. Simply having the intention to be famous or notorious is a very strange scam to pull on yourself.

We all know we can do whatever we want. I don't have to eat well today, but if not today, when? Will I wait until the pain arrives? It'll be more uncomfortable. Think ahead.

I try to live in the moment. I plan for the future but live in the present. Living in the present doesn't mean that I haven't set my sights, but there's no need to live in the tension of those sights. It's called 'do without doing'. It's straight out of the universe's magic box, but it takes a lot of trust. If you've made a statement of intent you can rest easy; it's in process. Do without doing. If you have put the intention out into the world, you'll naturally start acting towards it. If you've really decided to do something, a way will come. It's there, it's stated, and it's in the universe. But be careful what you intend to ask for, because you will get it.

If you do an unexpected and unnecessary act of kindness, the strange and wondrous thing is that the universe will always give you back a strange and unexpected act of kindness. It works like that. But it has to be done with the correct intention. Not with the expectation of getting it back.

16 Things

If I fall into a funk, I give myself 16 things to do. Moving the teacups into the dishwasher, washing up the saucepan, cleaning down the tiles, making the bed; all the way to 16. I could tell when a particular friend of mine was depressed because he'd always be immaculately presented. He'd say, 'I can't stop being depressed but at least I can do the ironing while I'm feeling down.' He used to make himself feel better by ironing his shirts.

Give yourself 16 things to do and then see how you feel when you walk out the door.

Be Positive and Have a Good Day

We use so many negative words. It's just a habit we get into. The habit of positivity can replace the habit of negativity. There's something cultural about it. We British love to tell stories that are both self-deprecating and end badly. 'I ended up in a field, in the mud, the car wouldn't start and it started raining' – the perfect end to a British story. I love telling a story in which I run myself down. It can be really funny, but what's not so good is to set that negative story for my day, or for my life, with that same self-deprecating gloom. It anticipates failure. We also have a problem with the way Americans seem to be so positive; it seems boastful. It's a bit like the way they say, 'Have a nice day.' At first I thought it sounded pretty hokey, but it's actually a good thing to say to someone and I don't see the problem now.

There's another whole box of tricks called NLP, Neuro-Linguistic Programming. In brief, it goes along with 'And the Word was made flesh.' What you say will manifest. It's the next step on from:

> *'As you think, so you are.*
> *As you imagine, so you become.'*

Positive intentions bring positive results.

Have a successful day. Make that decision early on. When you fire an arrow, you make the trajectory higher than where you know the arrow will fall. I set the sights on my tasks in a similar way.

MAP

The Co-Creative White Brotherhood Medical Assistance Program (MAP) is fascinating. It's a personal healing, diagnostic and wellness system that draws on the energy and wisdom of a collective of non-terrestrial beings known as 'The Ascended Masters' or 'Great White Brotherhood'. Despite the connotations of the name, the group includes both males and females and a rainbow of complexions. As I said before, I'm a spiritual bungee jumper. If it's not going to kill me or anyone else I'll try anything that's been recommended to me by a reliable source.

The MAP system involves lying down in a comfortable room, repeating an evocation that you read from a book to surround yourself with a protective field of psychic energy, and then calling on your personal medical assistance programme team. It sounded very unlikely when I first thought about trying it but when I did I was amazed to experience being visited by a French doctor, who looked incredibly like Agatha Christie's character, Hercule Poirot. When he appeared and started poking me I could feel it physically. There were other people with him. I noticed a very attractive woman among them. She looked as though she was in her early forties. Her hair was tied up and her styling suggested 1940s wartime.

'It's Mummy,' I suddenly thought. She turned to me in a manner that seemed to say, 'Yes, it is me.' 'Mummy, I've got to talk to you,' I said. 'I've desperately wanted to see you.' She looked at me as if to say, 'What's the problem?'

At the time I had a particularly challenging and sensitive family issue that was taking up a disproportionate amount of my energy. Her response was so contrary to what I would have said or thought myself, and so unexpected, it convinced me of MAP's truth and validity. She said things to me that I really didn't want to hear and found very hard to accept. They were far from what I would have 'made' her say if I'd been conjuring her up in my imagination.

I'm not sure if she said it, or simply communicated it to me, but she let me know that from where she was looking she could see that everything was perfect – exactly as it was meant to be and that I needn't be so concerned. She let me know that everyone was doing exactly what they were meant to be doing and that everything would be OK. It was really most odd.

What was strange, and interesting, was actually being able to physically feel the MAP team poking me. Whether they were actually there but in some parallel dimension, or being channelled through my imagination, I have no idea. What I do know is that the team diagnosed a problem with my right breast. I had a mammogram the next day which revealed a slight abnormality. Fortunately it didn't require surgery.

You can use the programme whenever you require some kind of medical assistance – be it physical or mental. I find the process enormously helpful and completely effective, and it was absolutely amazing to meet my mother as one of the great doctors in the sky.

The Last Thing

You might be thinking, 'Stephanie, all that really does sound totally preposterous and hokey Californian psychobabble.' But I'm someone who gets to work on time, knows my lines, and functions very well in the real world. When everything's going well I can tell you how to put on eyeliner and lipstick and what it's like to be a star in Hollywood, but life doesn't always go beautifully and we need to be able to help ourselves when we're down on the floor. I can also function even better if I'm maintaining a very different set of priorities to the ones I take on as commercial commitments – priorities that involve me exploring spiritual purpose. I'm only doing what the three psychics said I would. It wasn't clever of me to nearly end up seriously hurting somebody when I put destiny to the test, driving head-on towards that lorry. It's been worth slowly re-learning the way I think, and now I know I want to live the rest of my life happily and consciously.

Chapter Eleven

Aiming High

Being Humbly Arrogant

When we worked together, the wonderful Ron Lacey, who played the Nazi General in *Indiana Jones and the Raiders of the Lost Ark*, summed up the kind of character it took to work in our profession: 'Stephanie, the art of it is down to being able to be completely humble and utterly arrogant at the same time.' You have to be able to take criticism and rejection while maintaining the confidence to get up and try again, time and time again. The humility has to be real; the arrogance is just a confidence trick.

When I was working on *The Colbys* I took a couple of days out to do a Shakespeare symposium in Houston with Miriam Margolyes, Ian Ogilvy and John Neville. During the symposium John Neville recited Shakespeare's Sonnet 18 – better known as *Shall I compare thee to a summer's day?* He did it while looking straight into my eyes. It was incredibly beautiful. When we got back to Los Angeles, a limousine was waiting for me outside the airport. As I was getting in I noticed John standing at the bus stop. I asked him if he'd like a lift. 'No,' he replied, 'I'm fine.' 'You truly are,' I thought. It's only transport. Catching a bus will also get you home. When you're as consummately skilled as John Neville you don't need a limousine. It's just surface. Even after she'd become very successful, Maggie Smith used to catch the Tube.

I remember getting into a lift with Heather Chasen while we were doing the series *Marked Personal*. It was 1974 and we were both wearing fur coats. We looked at each other and started laughing. We knew the series was being axed and there we were, wearing the fabric of success. You have to stay humble, all the time fully believing you deserve your every success, and never getting out of the habit of catching the No. 23 bus.

Kindness

Kindness is so important. Ultimately, it's the greatest wisdom. When our mother died, my friends Philip and Steve took my sister Didi and me to Mexico. It was fabulous fun and, while we were there, because of the healing work they did with her, Didi felt safe enough to be able to let go and cry.

When you nurture others, you nurture yourself. Acts of generosity are actually quite selfish. When you do a good deed, you get back so much more. So be selfish – help a neighbour.

When I was 17 and working at the Liverpool Everyman I got sent to the laundrette with a big bag of laundry. I'd never been to a laundrette before. Walking in, I saw a tramp sitting in the corner with a bottle, talking to himself. I ran straight back to the theatre. I returned with someone to look after me. When we arrived they looked at the man and said, 'Hi, Tony.' Then they

Steve, me, Didi and Philip, disembarking from our holiday in Mexico

turned to me. 'Where's the tramp?' It was Anthony Hopkins with a bleach bottle, learning his lines. That was the first time we met.

When we were in Hong Kong, working together on *To Be the Best*, Anthony was taking the brave and fantastic step of stopping drinking, once and for all. I'd get the biggest yachts lined up for happy jaunts out, but he refused to come with us. 'Thank you, Stephanie,' he'd say, 'but something will annoy me and I know what I'll want to do – but I appreciate being invited.'

Some years later I was at a big charity event for the Coen brothers. Holly Hunter had given a speech, then Sigourney Weaver had followed that, and then the prize for the raffle was drawn. I won it. I was thrilled. 'How lovely,' I thought. I went up to the stage and suddenly realized it was like winning a scratch card at the Oscars. I didn't know what to do. All I could say was 'Thank you' before turning and going back down the stairs. It felt so humiliating. Anthony Hopkins was sitting at a table right in front of the stage. He saw my embarrassment, got up from his seat and, as I was coming down the stairs, walked straight up to me.

'Stephanie!' he exclaimed. 'How wonderful to see you again, how are you?'

'Embarrassed' I said, looking distraught.

'That's all right,' he said, taking me by the arm. 'Now, where are you sitting?' He accompanied me to my table. When we got there, I told him how grateful I was. 'Whenever you need help,' he said to me, with absolute sincerity, 'I'm here for you.' I was incredibly touched. How generous was that? Anthony had seen my embarrassment and had had the kindness to come to my aid. He was such a knight.

When I was working on *Venice Preserv'd* at the National Theatre, just before my near-death experience, I discovered how magnanimous Ian McKellen is.

During rehearsals Ian was coming through these enormous doors and going straight upstage. He'd be facing the audience and I'd be facing him. By doing that, he'd have the audience's full attention and all they'd see of me was my back. I was being upstaged by Ian McKellen. I thought, 'OK, thanks,' and asked Alison Chitty, the designer, to add a 15-foot train to my costume. 'A 15-foot train behind you?' she said. 'You'll never manage.'

'I will, darling,' I assured her. 'It's the only thing about me anyone's going to notice because Ian's going straight in upstage.' 'Really?' she asked.

'Honestly,' I replied. '15 feet, please. Give them something to look at.'

We got to the first preview and burst on-stage through the door. I felt suddenly warmed by the fact that we were out of the rehearsal room. I was so relieved there were real people, ordinary people wearing cardigans, sitting in the audience. We made our entrance and Ian went upstage. I delivered my line and got a laugh. Ian came downstage. We continued the scene and I got another laugh. Ian went even further downstage. Now I was facing the audience. I thought, 'OK, this is good. Hello, audience.' I was playing with my long train, swirling it around and really enjoying myself.

We came to the second preview and, when we burst through the big doors, Ian didn't go upstage. He went across it instead, and I got my laughs. Ian moved downstage and I got more laughs.

It was opening night. We burst through the doors and Ian went straight downstage. I was getting all my laughs and suddenly it made total sense. What Ian McKellen does is, if he thinks he has to hold the scene together, he'll go upstage and give the audience as much as he can. If he thinks the other actors are pulling their weight, or more than pulling their weight, he's generosity itself. He'll give the scene to his fellow actors. He's fabulous. His first thought was for the audience, but I was a close second. He needed to feel confident I'd be able to step up to the mark, but once he saw I could, he gave me the stage. It became my scene; given to me by now *Sir* Ian McKellen – and 'Sir', rightly so.

Robert Powell is another generous actor. I've worked with him several times. I once told him that, if we carried on down-staging each other, one of us was likely to fall off the stage. Another time I walked on stage, began the scene, then came out with 'Pah, rubbish' and walked off again. I started the scene again, as if doing a second take. I didn't miss a beat and neither did Robert. Afterwards, with his lovely laugh, all he said was, 'That was interesting'. Robert is love and generosity itself.

My sister Didi is a kind and warm person. It's why people are so drawn to her. A few months after Bill, her wonderful husband of more than 40 years, had died, my dear friend Prince Azim of Brunei invited us to Brunei for a holiday. He thought it would be good for Didi. We went, and it helped Didi enormously with her grieving process. Prince Azim is another amazingly kind and generous person.

At a charity dinner with Prince Azim and Al Gore

Consciousness

I used to be afraid of the word 'consciousness'. It sounded a bit like attempting a Full Lotus position. Then I realized that all it meant was being aware of what was going on. If you're aware then you're looking, and if you're really looking at a situation you can work out what's actually going on. Once you're doing that, if you need a solution you'll be able to see one.

There's a bit of a contradiction between the spiritual books that tell you to live consciously in the moment and the basic truth of simple housekeeping, which demands that you have to plan ahead. The past is over but the present informs tomorrow. In Western societies it's only really possible to live in the moment if you have a great deal of money; otherwise you need to plan ahead. You've got to be practical, but it's also important not to let the practicalities become overwhelming. I make sure I take time out to see something of beauty every day. I read a poem, laugh with a friend, or brush my dogs with love and care. In their own way these things are beautiful.

Once you're conscious you're lumbered – there is no option not to be. If you behave in an unconscious fashion, the universe will slap you down.

Being conscious also means being able to see things as they are – without any preconceived opinions or judgement. It's hard not to make a judgement or want to control a situation.

I was on the beach with Phoebe when she was about three. While she was digging sandcastles, a little boy and his mother walked past. Phoebe looked up. This little chap had a hand that came directly out of his shoulder. She went straight over to him. Embarrassed, I started apologizing to the boy's mother. 'Oh, no,' she said. 'He loves to show it off.' The little guy had a great audience in Phoebe; he loved the attention. Phoebe thought having a hand stuck on your shoulder was the coolest thing. She was far too young to think anything cruel. She was just interested to see something she'd never ever come across before. She accepted the boy for what he was rather than thinking she'd prefer him to be otherwise. Little children are *so* aware of how to be. That taught me something.

Animals

I've been using animals to help me for a long time. Fox has always been a good guide for me. He certainly helped me work out how I was going to deal with Pam Ferris' character while we were rehearsing *Connie*. Sometimes I'll be in a stressful situation and I'll feel it would be good to be able to call on a higher power to help me, but I'm thinking, 'I don't have a stinking higher power. I've got a thumping headache – I'm stuck in Oxford Street and I can't lift my feet off the ground, let alone get in touch with my higher power.' Animal guides come into their own under these sorts of conditions. I'll make a little evocation and ask fox, crow or eagle to show me the way.

Fox is cunning, but with humour and always with a smile. Fox will show you alternative ways of approaching a situation. Crow is law. Crow reminds us to stay in line with the process. Crow reminds us that the universe has laws, and that there are consequences to our going against them.

If I'm losing objectivity I'll ask eagle for help. Being able to see things from 30 feet up gives you an entirely different perspective. Things always look very different when you can see them from above. When we're confronted by difficulty we need to fly like an eagle rather than be petrified like a rabbit or mouse. Eagle is good for big problems. You're not actually going to be able to mend a child's toy as eagle – you need mouse for that, attention to detail – but you will be able to get the perspective you need to be able to sort out a situation.

We have God nature and we have animal nature. And it's because we're so intelligent that we can be so vicious. Our animal nature encompasses a selfishness that is exclusive of other people's survival, but our God nature realizes that other people *are* our survival. Fear invokes the animal instinct for self-preservation. If we could rise above it all like eagle, and see the true nature of everything, we'd see that it all makes sense, and avoid getting snared by fear.

One day, soon after I'd turned 50, I was watching a report on television that recommended people of my age get tested for a particular medical procedure. 'Not likely,' I thought. 'I'm not going to do that.' All of a sudden I heard a terrible rattling coming from the room next door. I went to look and saw a dove careening around. It took me ages to get it out, but eventually I managed. I looked it up in my animal book. Dove is messenger. I thought it best I follow up on the report I'd been watching. I got tested. I needed the procedure.

A week later I heard a much more gentle fluttering sound coming from the same room. I went to see what it was. A beautiful little hummingbird was hovering around the room. Hummingbirds rarely fly into houses; they stay outside, flying where there's nectar. There was nothing in my living room that might have attracted it. When I went into the room to say 'hello', it flew around for a moment or two and then flew out. I looked it up. Hummingbird is joy.

Grace

Once when I was in China I saw two old men at opposite ends of a street sweeping in perfect rhythm and total harmony. They were carrying out a simple task, but with such beauty and grace.

The same food can be slopped onto a plate or presented well and with grace – it makes such a difference. Grace is another of those words that needs to be taken off the 'Only for Saints' shelf, scrubbed down with a bit of Ajax and allowed to live brightly in all our lives.

Grace is about attitude; it's in the detail and is very practical. Grace includes gratitude; it's a blessing, and it involves doing things with good intention. To do something with grace means doing it with awareness. Grace could have all these words flowing in her skirt. It's one of those things you know when you see it. Lucifer's angels were banished from heaven in disgrace.

Working with Bill Roache on *Coronation Street* in 2009 was a lesson in grace. It was an extraordinary period for both of us, and I sincerely believe we were put together to ride out that particular time in our lives. While we had a very gentle story line together on *Coronation Street*, our lives away from work were quite challenging.

I started the job in the depths of a personal crisis. My daughter Phoebe wasn't well and my grandson Jude's situation was uncertain. Everything felt rather insecure. It was great that I was working in the UK, but my personal circumstances were difficult. Bill was a very good person to be working with – very solid and stabilizing. Then his wife died, very suddenly and quite unexpectedly. Although we share a belief that death is not the end, it was terribly sad. The whole *Coronation Street* family shared much unspoken communication, empathy and, in the nicest sense, love.

Over the years I've worked with a host of international stars, and I can truly say that the quality of Bill's spirit is as bright as any I've met in that time.

It All Cross-Checks

Apart from her offering Earl Grey tea to Ken Barlow a little too often, I felt quite an affinity for Martha, the character I played in *Coronation Street*. She was educated, not demanding and a good, strong, independent woman. As I've got older, different aspects of my life have come closer together.

In one of my earliest interviews, when I was just starting out as an actress, I said I'd been born in Casablanca. That established the distance I've maintained between how I've chosen to represent myself and who I am. Since the Casablanca story, rather than continuing to stretch the truth, I've tended to limit it. My private persona has always been very different to my public persona. I'm an actress. I've developed a character I use when I turn up for interviews and publicity. Though it's meant I've been tarred with my own brush. I'm most happy remaining anonymous and just being left to play. It's easy for people who know my work to imagine me very differently from who I really am. That's why my true friends are so important to me.

A lot of the characters I've played have had a toxic energy, with inflated and wounded egos. So I always enjoy being able to play a really nasty piece of work as comedy. For the most part, that's what Amanda Barrie and I did with our characters in *Bad Girls*. We didn't take our Costa cons seriously; they were a wicked pair of con artists but we were far more interested in lying on our backs listening to Radio 4 in our dressing room. And our characters seemed to work. We never knew why, never bothered to find out. We just got on with it. We didn't get too engaged.

Sometimes you have to get engaged, however. The energy you have to use is strong, but not necessarily good. It's why having a spiritual practice is so valuable. It allows me to deflate, to re-align and find harmony again – to breathe out those false, damaged characters. Making sure I remove my make-up has always been part of the ritual. Katharine Ross' daughter Cleo used to call it 'make-muck'. Washing off the make-muck has always been important. I really don't want to take home the characters I play.

Amanda Barrie and me

I don't understand longing for fame, but I do cherish being good at something. Talent isn't mine, it's a gift for me to hold and treasure, and to feed with what it needs. We should feed our gifts like little birds who've alighted on our hands. Feed and house them; they've been given to us to care for. It's so easy to squander our talents, but they're like flames that should be built into a big fire, not left to burn out or be doused with drink.

Don't look sideways; just know what you want and go for it. We are not in competition with other people. We all have different challenges, different demons. Enjoy being inspired by others' success stories.

In my experience the universe gives us more of what we're paying attention to, so it's a good idea to want what that is. Go for what you want and work until you get it. If you didn't get the job you went for today, you'll get something else. All you can ever do is to be fully prepared and fully open to all possibilities, and if you don't do so well this time, make up your mind to do better next time. You might not be able to change your circumstances, but you can change your attitude.

Chapter Twelve

The Contract

One Life, Many Lives

Eventually, the pieces all join together – it all becomes one in the end.

It's like our lives: they all join together, too. We're all in the same struggle, and we're all part of the same perfection. Though, like sunshine and clouds, we often become temporarily disconnected from our purpose. We know the truth but then we fall away, flawed species that we are. The joy and love on the face of a baby is complete – before they have ego, before they individualize, before they fall away, before they separate out and adapt to the deep loneliness of atomized existence.

Before we fall away we know there is one life that runs through you, me and everything that exists. That life is what we call God. One life; one energy. It's also called love. It was the truth I realized on the rooftop at RADA. It has little to do with religion.

We are spirit in body, and our spirit is the perfect gift of God. We *are* love.

I believe our souls leave an energetic imprint – a record of this lifetime. Imagine a vast data-bank in which you could find the records for every human life that has ever been. In the same library you'd be able to access detailed information about the history of the universe. Constantly being updated, it's an information repository for each of our many lives. It's there, somewhere out in the ether.

Malibu

Rising from the Pacific Ocean and sweeping to the heavens above, the Santa Monica Mountains form the scenic backdrop to my life now. When I wake, their sharp ridges and deep canyons frame the rising sun; and at dusk, together with my dogs we watch a golden disc drop into the horizon far beyond the rolling surf.

If I could lay out my life along the water's edge and soar in the sky like the mountains' eagles, I'd see a jigsaw; no longer messy pieces of a puzzle but a remarkable tapestry. Our lives are a blessing we stitch together, from moment to moment and life to life.

I love to sew, to paint, and to play with clay. Sometimes I make clay jigsaw puzzles and fire them. Sometimes some of the pieces go a bit awry in the corners because they're clay, and unpredictable. That's how my life would appear as I soared over it: unpredictable, and with tricky edges, but joined up perfectly in God's grand scheme.

Barnet

I came into this life in Southgate, North London, in 1947; emerging from the ashes of the Second World War and born on the cusp of a new age.

I can remember my amusement at having feet, of wearing shoes, of walking and running – of being in body. I loved the whole experience, my appreciation heightened by a lingering memory-trace of what it was like to be without body. If there was a wall, I had to walk on it. If there was a window, I had to climb out of it. My friend Heather and I would never do the simple thing and just go to the cupboard where my mother kept the biscuits. That wasn't enough. We'd go round to her house and sneak into the living room where her mother kept a glass canister full of biscuits. We'd help ourselves and then escape with our loot by climbing through the lavatory window, jumping onto the garage roof and sliding down a drainpipe. It felt glorious to be physical, to have a body, and to play.

About seven years old, sitting in the garden at home

Angels

I've already mentioned my flying angel friends. I've always known about angels and I've always loved them. Before falling asleep I'd say a prayer: 'Matthew, Mark, Luke and John, bless this bed I lay upon, two angels at my head, two angels at my feet, now I lay me down to sleep.' The Virgin Mary had angels, and my mother had an angel that looked after her, too.

She was going to visit a friend who was in trouble and needed her help. She was at a railway station, very weary and struggling with her suitcase. She was about to faint. Suddenly, a tall young man with blond hair appeared at her side. 'Let me help you with that,' he said, taking her suitcase. She didn't utter a word, yet he knew which platform, which train and which carriage to take her to. Then he disappeared. The next time she saw him it's possible he saved her life. She was travelling on a coach, sitting very close to the driver. What happened next took place in an instant. The driver had a heart attack and slumped in his seat. Mummy saw him drop and prayed hard. Suddenly, the young man who'd helped her at the railway station was there. He brought the coach to a halt and disappeared.

I used to make spirit puppets for the charity Free Arts for Abused Children. I'd spend a day with young children who'd been put in institutions because their parents were constantly at war with each other, or on death row, or for some other reason that had led to them being taken away from their home. They're bitter children. There's nothing better than meeting a grumpy kid at the start of the morning and then, at the end of a day of art, getting a big painty kiss and a hug.

A spirit puppet is just a clump of newspaper wrapped in Plaster of Paris bandage on top of a stick, with another stick going crossways for arms, dressed with bits of scrap material and painted over. It's a guardian angel. When we start making them, the children usually think their angels have to be white with blonde hair. I'd explain otherwise. We've ended up making yellow angels, green angels, turquoise angels, angels that look like Diana Ross and angels that look like Michael Jackson. I'd ask them what their angels did. Some were angel doctors who could mend mummy and others were angel astronauts who could take them far away. We'd stick them in the ground and I'd get them to make a wish. You're not there to be a psychiatrist; you're there to do the dirty work of painting, gluing and sticking-together. Give a child the idea that they have a guardian angel and, guess what, they have one. Tell them they can talk to it, and they will. Introduce them to the realm of possibilities and they'll fly with it. Making guardian angels with children for the day; that's practical spirituality. Free Arts is a beautiful thing; it's one of my favourite charities. I've done lots of fundraisers for them. I get a lot more out than I put in. Be really selfish, go and do a Free Arts day.

Interlife

I knew about angels before I came here. When I was under hypnosis, during a session of 'soul memory research', I experienced a memory-trace of grey-and-white wings and of being in the middle of a discussion. I was saying that I didn't want to go back to being in a body. I didn't think I needed to go back and lead another life but was being gently told I must.

The hypnotherapist I worked with is based in North Hollywood. She believes we carry memories that go way beyond this life – memories we can draw on to make better sense of the life we're living now. She studied with Dr Michael Newton, the original pioneer of 'soul memory research'. Through his work as a hypnotherapist Dr Newton helped clients uncover memories of a dimension beyond, or parallel to, the physical one we inhabit. Uncovering more and more evidence of a spirit world from which souls pass into life in the physical dimension, he started outlining what he called the 'interlife' – a realm of 'life before life'. Under hypnosis, I discovered that I came into this life with a contract. It's ironic that I've signed contracts for each job I've ever done in my life – hundreds of them – signing up for a few hours a day, a week, or a year; sub-clauses initialled after the back and forth of negotiation of fine points. I've never been on a permanent contract with the RSC, National Theatre or a film or television company. I've had so many contracts; some brilliant, some fun, some a big compromise – all individual jobs, one after another. I've been a negotiator and a barterer, I make deals; it's how I came into this life. I didn't want to come in at all. I didn't want to leave the realm of spirits and angels. So I made a deal. I'd only go back to the physical realm if I was born into comfort; with all the necessary ingredients of living to make it a happy and good life – good parents, a good family, good looks and success. They were the terms agreed. But what would be the point if not to learn? My contract had an unexpected twist.

Under hypnosis, I felt myself slip into a collection of cells, vessels and tissue. Blue angels were laughing and darting across my vision as I fitted into a transparent shell that sheathed me in opaqueness. My transition to the corporeal was heralded by jokes and kindness, sweet peals of laughter and bells. The angels were celebrating.

At first it was warm and comforting, then it changed and the host body became a vile place to be. There were spots in the liquid I was floating in. It felt disgusting and contaminated. Something was wrong. The host body was unwell. My mother had chicken pox. As a result I was born with no hearing in my right ear and only 80 per cent in my left.

Steph's Deaf

In one version of my story I have an idyllic childhood, cocooned in the secure and predictable environment of an English middle-class suburban life. In this version my mother loves me unconditionally. When she was very old I realized there'd been another version. It was closer to the truth. The reality of her unconditional love had been otherwise. Towards the end of her life I started to see how extremely controlling and judgemental she was. I realized she'd always been like that. It made me think that the unconditional love that I'd thought I'd given to my own children was just as conditional as my mother's had been to me. I'd probably been just as controlling, too. I remember wanting to go to tap-dancing lessons and wear a wrap-around angora top – I wasn't allowed. My mother had too much good taste.

Needing to be able to maintain tight control, if anything slipped beyond her grasp – including when she encountered something she couldn't do anything about, as far as she was concerned – it would cease to exist. And that's what she did with my hearing impairment.

I only have mono hearing – I don't hear in stereo. I've no sense whatsoever of where sounds come from, so I nearly get run over on a daily basis. A specialist explained it in terms of painting. He explained that my hearing is similar to a primitive painting. There's no perspective, it's a flat canvas; an object at the bottom of the canvas is on the same plane as an object in the middle. In hearing terms, it means a faraway sound enters my perception without sounding far away. Parties are hell. If I'm on the telephone and the person I'm speaking to has noise in the background I can't continue with the call, and if someone in the room speaks to me while I'm on the phone, I can't hear them.

Working in the theatre brings a whole set of challenges. Working out the acoustics of a new venue is just one of them. Working out how much projection an auditorium requires takes the assistance of another person. I usually ask one of the cast to speak to me from the back of the theatre, and then to listen to me delivering a line or two. I learned an invaluable technique from my wonderful voice teacher, Kate Flemming, at RADA; I still use it today. She taught me what's called 'rib reserve breathing'. Basically it involves keeping your ribs out the whole time and grabbing breath to fill your lungs without moving them. When the person listening to me from the back of the theatre thinks the level of my voice is right, I repeat the line using the same amount of breath. If they say it sounds good, I know how much breath to use to produce the right level of sound for that auditorium. A voice check in a new venue is important to all actors; to me, it's vital. When I'm being fitted for a corset I have to remember to swing my ribs out while I'm being measured. On film it's different, then I just say, 'Torture me, I don't care, I want to look thin.'

When I was a child it took a while for my parents to notice that something was wrong with my hearing and, when they realized it wasn't right, they did what they could. I had test after test, then I had my adenoids out. After that, my parents didn't know what else to do. As far as my mother was concerned, I wasn't deaf any more and the subject was closed. I still had to live with it. Reciting the 'Hail Mary' at the convent school, instead of, 'Hail Mary, full of grace, The Lord is with thee, Blessed art thou among women, And blessed is the fruit of thy womb, Jesus,' I heard, 'Hello Mary, full of grease, blessed is your fruity womb.'

My classmates thought it was hilarious when it was my turn to recite the prayer. I was teased terribly at school.

In some ways, maybe my mother's approach was brilliant parenting. My lack of hearing was never used as an excuse for not achieving at school, but it had more of an effect on me than was ever realized – particularly its denial. It was as if I wasn't accepted for the person I really was.

It took me years to stop being ashamed of being deaf. I hid it. When I couldn't hear, I would pretend to be bored with the conversation and, rather than lean in and lip-read, I would try to look aloof. I excluded myself. I left myself out. I didn't want to be part of the deaf community, either. Deaf people had speech impediments, were the brunt of jokes and were thought to be slow on the uptake. I refused to learn sign language, too, even though I was warned I might lose all hearing by the time I was 21. I was in as much denial as my mother.

As I got older I learned to compensate, but it took years for me to be able to ask people to be on my left side, in order to be able to hear them speak. I remember people thinking I was coy, or getting the wrong idea because I'd be looking intently at them while they were speaking. I knew I needed help but it wasn't something I could bring up, because my deafness wasn't acknowledged. I felt alienated.

Listening is very tiring for a person with a hearing loss. We have to fill in a lot of the blanks to follow the gist of what's being said. When someone covers their mouth with their hands we can't hear what they're saying because we won't be able to read their lips. I've made friends laugh because I've not heard the last thing they said; which might have been to do with a completely different subject but I've replied as if they were still talking about their original topic. It's funny among friends, but my hearing loss can make me feel panicky at an airport or train station. I can't hear anything over a tannoy if there are other sounds around me. I can't tell where individual sounds are coming from, I just hear a wall of indistinguishable noise.

Deaf people seek quiet places. That might sound odd, but they're the only places we can hear with any clarity. I love to visit with friends, one on one, in a park or at home; never in a popular noisy restaurant. As deafness increases, sociability decreases. We're upset at not being able to hear and are annoying to communicate with. It's a slow spiral to isolation.

I have two charities that I support with all my might. One is Sense, and the other is Hearing Dogs for the Deaf.

Sense supports deafblind people. One really important thing the charity does is assist people in communicating with their hearing-impaired relatives and friends. A tiny and sweet example might be to offer a deafblind person a cup of tea by taking their hand and writing the letter 'T' on it, and watching for a response. We're deaf, not stupid. We don't want big embarrassing mime acts. We don't want big anything. We definitely don't want to be shouted at.

Deafness can be very lonely. I'm fortunate that I'm happy in my own company. I actually need to spend a lot of time alone. Listening is exhausting. I'm also fortunate that I have a job in which I know what the other people are saying – because of the script. I know when I'm getting tired; I start to talk too much. That way I don't have to listen so much. Being with my dogs is a way that I can be in company and not get tired. Everyone knows what amazing companions animals can be; imagine having one that listens for you. A hearing dog will let you know when the telephone is ringing or when someone is at the door; it will wake you up when the alarm goes in the morning and, to top it all, it'll be your best friend. A hearing dog can be any size or any breed, though mongrels tend to be the most intelligent. I've known some scruffy little mutts who have turned their owner's lives around – even saved their lives. The dogs seem to know it, too; the right pairing of a trained hearing dog and its master is a close and very moving friendship.

My mother did the best she could, based on what she knew and on her own personality. Making it up as we go along, what more can we do as parents? I started out as a novice, we all do, but ultimately my children have been my greatest teachers. As if looking in a mirror, I see myself reflected back from them. I'm forever indebted, for where would I be without them? It's such a complex and difficult challenge, such a beautiful and humbling experience. Maybe we get wise by the time we're grandparents.

My contract's twist, which was not negotiated, was my hearing loss. There were the wonderful absolutes of the 1950s and then I just rode the crest of the wave. But it would have been like that – it was in my contract. I always found myself in the right place at the right time, but I would have; that was what I'd negotiated. The only thing I hadn't been told was that I was going to come into this life deaf. But how good is that? What would the point to coming back have been if there wasn't an edge?

I was hosting an award ceremony for the National Council for Communicative Disorders in Washington, D.C. Earlier that day I'd been to the Holocaust Museum; it had recently opened. I felt a bit anxious because I hadn't written my opening speech, but I really wanted to see this new museum. The speech wrote itself. I realized that, had I lived in Nazi Germany, I would have been killed – like anybody else with an impairment. Instead, I was able to welcome a deaf Miss America onto the stage of the John F. Kennedy Center to congratulate her for overcoming her disability and to celebrate her success. That was a good feeling.

It was through the National Council of Communicative Disorders that I met Senator John Glenn and his wife Annie. How can you have an astronaut as a friend? This life is extraordinarily bountiful. It's the munificence of the life I've been given. It has included an impairment that's offered me a very particular insight and a grasp on humanity. An impairment can be an asset. It's an area in which I feel responsible.

I'm so lucky to have come so far from when I was a little girl who couldn't hear very well, who wouldn't answer to 'Steph', because 'Steph's deaf'; all the way to becoming a well-known actress who's proud to spread a better understanding of deafness. I'm no longer ashamed of my impairment, but proud of my success.

It's been a long journey.

List of Film, TV and Theatre Work

Show name	Character	Year	Type
ELECTRA	Electra	1962	Q.E.G.S Barnet
HENRY IV	Lady Mortimer	1964–1965	Liverpool Everyman
SERVANT OF TWO MASTERS	Clarice	1964–1965	Liverpool Everyman
MACBETH	First Witch	1964–1965	Liverpool Everyman
TOAD OF TOAD HALL	Marigold and Phoebe	1964–1965	Liverpool Everyman
THE MERCHANT OF VENICE	Portia	1965	RADA
TWELFTH NIGHT	Maria	1965	RADA
OEDIPUS	Jocasta	1966	RADA
THREE SISTERS	Irena	1966	RADA
GUYS AND DOLLS	Doll	1967	RADA
MONSIEUR BARNETT	Yasmina	1967	Bristol, Old Vic Theatre
THE MADWOMAN OF CHAILLOT	Irma	1967	Oxford Playhouse Theatre tour
THE QUEEN'S TRAITOR	Mary, Queen of Scots	1967	TV serial
ARMS AND THE MAN	Louka	1968	Oxford Playhouse
GASLIGHT	Nancy	1968	Oxford Playhouse
THE SILENT WOMAN	Mavis	1968	Oxford Playhouse
GOING FOR A SONG	as myself	1968	BBC Bristol
BON VOYAGE	Lisa Wendle	1968	ITV Playhouse
THE SAINT	Penelope Brown	1968	Guest, TV series
THE JAZZ AGE	Charlotte Tonn	1968	BBC serial
LOVE STORY	Linda	1969	Armchair Theatre, TV
PUBLIC EYE	Shirley Marlowe	1969	Guest, TV series
THE DISTRACTED PREACHER	Lizzy Newberry	1969	TV film
TAM LIN/THE DEVIL'S WIDOW	Janet Ainsley	1969	Feature film
THE NIGHTCOMERS	Miss Jessel	1970	Feature film
THE BASEMENT	Jane	1970	Duchess Theatre, London
TEA PARTY	Wendy	1970	Duchess Theatre, London
UFO	Sarah Bosanquet	1970	Guest, TV series
SENTIMENTAL EDUCATION	Rosanette	1970	BBC serial
THE GAMES	Angela Simmonds	1970	Feature film
CALLAN	Beth Lampton	1970	Guest, TV series
THE TEMPEST	Juno	1971	Nottingham Playhouse

Show name	Character	Year	Type
THE HOMECOMING	Ruth	1971	Nottingham Playhouse
A DOLL'S HOUSE	Nora Helmer	1971	Nottingham Playhouse
ITV SATURDAY NIGHT	Anna Trenton / Jenny Draper	1971–1972	TV play
MAN AT THE TOP	Paula Fraser	1972	Guest, TV series
DRACULA A.D. 1972	Jessica Van Helsing	1972	Feature film
JASON KING	Cora Simpson	1972	Guest, TV series
EGO HUGO	Adele Hugo	1973	TV movie
JANE EYRE	Blanche Ingram	1973	BBC serial
SPECIAL BRANCH	Sue Arden	1973	Guest, TV series
AND NOW THE SCREAMING STARTS!	Catherine Fengriffen	1973	Feature film
THE PROTECTORS	Chrissie	1973	Guest, TV series
MAFIA JUNCTION	Joanne	1973	Feature film
THE ADVENTURER	Contessa Maria	1973	Guest, TV series
MARKED PERSONAL	Georgina Layton	1973–1974	TV series
THE CONFESSIONAL	Vanessa Welch	1974	Feature film
NAPOLEON AND LOVE	Madame Duchatel	1974	TV serial
PROMETHEUS: THE LIFE	Fanny Lovell	1975	TV mini-series
ON APPROVAL	Helen Hayle	1976	Theatre Royal Haymarket, London
SCHIZO	Beth	1976	Feature film
FORGET ME NOT	Jeanne Teliot	1976	Guest, TV series
HADLEIGH	Susan Debray	1976	Guest, TV series
ABSURD PERSON SINGULAR	Eva Jackson	1977	Theatre, Coventry
I VECCHI E I GIOVANI	Nicoletta	1977	TV mini-series
THE LONDON CUCKOLDS	Eugenia Dashwell	1978	Royal Court Theatre, London
RAINBOW	Special Guest Narrator	1978	Guest, TV series
THE SINGULAR LIFE OF ALBERT NOBBS	Hubert Page	1978	New End Theatre, Hampstead, London
AN AUDIENCE CALLED EDOUARD	Berthe	1978	Greenwich Theatre, London
CAN YOU HEAR ME AT THE BACK?	Margery Hartnoll	1979	Piccadilly Theatre, London
HORROR PLANET	Kate	1981	Feature film
TENKO	Rose Millar	1981–1982	TV series
TERRA NOVA	Kathleen Scott	1982	Watford Theatre
TWELFTH NIGHT	Olivia	1983	Theatre

Show name	Character	Year	Type
HAPPY FAMILY	Deborah Solstice	1983	Duke of York's Theatre, London
VENICE PRESERV'D	Aquilina	1984	National Theatre, London
SORRELL AND SON	Florence Palfrey	1984	TV mini-series
CONNIE	Connie	1985	TV series
DYNASTY	Sable Colby	1985–1989	TV series
THE COLBYS	Sable Scott Colby	1985–1987	TV series
THE LOVE BOAT	Elaine Riskin	1986	Guest appearance, TV
FOX MYSTERY THEATER	Rosemary Richardson	1986	Guest appearance, TV
NAPOLEON AND JOSEPHINE: A LOVE STORY	Therese Tallien	1987	TV mini-series
THE ROVER	Angelica Bianca	1988	Royal Shakespeare Company
FRENCH AND SAUNDERS	Doreena Petherbridge	1988	Guest appearance, TV
THE WOLVES OF WILLOUGHBY CHASE	Letitia Slighcarp	1989	Feature film
TROOP BEVERLY HILLS	Vicki Sprantz	1989	Feature film
SISTER KATE	Sister Kate	1989–1990	TV series
LUCKY CHANCES	Susan Martino Santangelo	1990	TV mini-series
CLUEDO	Mrs. Peacock	1990	TV series
HARRY AND HARRIET	Christine Pertersen	1990	Feature film
THE LILAC BUS	Judy	1990	TV movie
THE VORTEX	Florence Lancaster	1991	Theatre, Los Angeles
BEVERLY HILLS, 90210	Iris McKay	1991–1994	Regular, TV series
TO BE THE BEST	Arabella	1992	TV movie
SECRETS	Sabina Quarles	1992	TV movie
LOVE LETTERS	Melissa Gardner	1992–1993	Canon Theater, Los Angeles
BLOSSOM	Mrs. Robinson	1993	Guest, TV series
RIDERS	Molly Carter	1993	TV series
FOREIGN AFFAIRS	Rosemary Radley	1993	TV movie
STAR TREK: THE NEXT GENERATION	Countess Bartholomew	1993	TV series
SEAQUEST DSV	Kristin Westphalen	1993–1994	TV series
A CHANGE OF PLACE	Marie	1994	TV movie
BURKE'S LAW	Victoria Lancer	1994	Guest, TV series
THE FATHER	Laura	1995	Theatre tour
HIGH SOCIETY	Stella, the acting Coach	1995	Guest, TV series
LEGEND	Vera Slaughter	1995	Guest, TV series

Show name	Character	Year	Type
WEDDING BELL BLUES	Tanya's Mother	1996	Feature film
NO BANANAS	Dorothea Grant	1996	BBC series
AN IDEAL HUSBAND	Mrs. Cheveley	1997–1999	Theatre – Broadway and Australia
EQUALLY DIVIDED	Renata	1998	Theatre tour
FUNNY ABOUT LOVE	Rosie	1999	Theatre tour
A BUSY DAY	Lady Wilhelmina Tylney	2000	Lyric Theatre, London
RELATIVE VALUES	Elizabeth	2000	Feature film
CHARMED	Martha van Lewen	2000	Guest appearance, TV
AN IDEAL HUSBAND	Mrs. Cheveley	2001	Papermill Playhouse, New Jersey
NOBODY'S PERFECT	Harriet Copland	2001–2002	Theatre tour
WOULD I LIE TO YOU?	Amaelia	2002	Feature film
ELIZABETH REX	Elizabeth I	2002	Birmingham Rep
UNCONDITIONAL LOVE	Harriet Fox-Smith	2002	Feature film
HAVING IT OFF	Vernice Green	2002	Guest appearance, TV
BAD GIRLS	Phyllida Oswyn	2003–2006	TV Series
DINNER	Paige	2004	Theatre tour
LOVE AND OTHER DISASTERS	Felicity Riggs-Wentworth	2006	Feature film
THE WITCHES HAMMER	Medline	2006	Feature film
NEW TRICKS	Rhoda Wishaw	2006	Guest, TV series
SEVEN DAYS OF GRACE	Dana	2006	Feature film
SNOW WHITE AND THE SEVEN DWARFS	Wicked Queen	2006–2007	Theatre, Guildford
STRICTLY COME DANCING	as myself	2007	BBC TV series
HAY FEVER	Judith Bliss	2007	Theatre tour
JACK AND THE BEANSTALK	Venus Flytrap, The Wicked Fairy	2007–2008	Theatre, Guildford
PLOT 7	Emma Osterman	2008	Feature film
FREE AGENTS	Wendy	2009	Guest appearance, TV
CORONATION STREET	Martha Fraser	2009–2010	TV series
CELEBRITY BIG BROTHER	as myself	2010	Reality TV series
MATERIAL GIRL	Sylvie Montrose	2010	Guest appearance, TV
MASTER CLASS	Maria Callas	2010–2011	Theatre Royal, Bath, and Chichester Festival Theatre tour

Index

Acknowledgments

I had no idea when I started this book just how much I would have to learn and how inadequate for the task I was. I would like to thank Owen Smith for holding my hand and never being condescending. Thank you Michelle Pilley, for being such a believer and cheerleader, and everyone at Hay House for their help. Thank you Natasha G. for pulling stuff out of me, and thank you Bill Roache for being so kind and generous.

As for the people around me every day I should like to apologize for being such a needy friend. Thank you Angie Milliken, for helping me with everything that had a plug attached to it, especially my laptop. Without you I would have thrown it out of the window in frustration. Thank you, darling Bernie Greenwood, for not having thrown me out of the window, and for staying by my side, always with good advice.

Patti Nicolella, your help and friendship makes everything possible, and Colin Horowitz, without your love and criticism I would be lost. Thank you Judy Geeson, for your beautiful photographs, and Wendy Murray for your wisdom, and Helen Campanella for being you. I would like to thank Maureen Vincent for her never-ending laconic encouragement, and lastly Jude Penny whose summer holiday was vastly compromised but who never complained. I love you all.

In conjunction with
Many Lives
Phase Eight is offering you

20% discount

in Phase Eight stores and online
at www.phase-eight.co.uk

Phase Eight is a nationwide
boutique style clothing chain that
is the perfect one-stop shopping
destination for all your fashion
needs. Whether you are looking
for a fabulous outfit for that special
occasion, or simply want to refresh
and update your existing wardrobe
staples, Phase Eight has fashion
that will take you anywhere.

**Simply take your voucher with you
on your next shopping trip to
redeem or head to the Phase Eight
website and enter the code below.**

Offer ends 14th November 2011

Phase Eight

20% discount

To claim your discount in store please present the voucher when
making your purchase at any Phase Eight stand-alone store.

To redeem the discount online please enter the promo code
8SBW when prompted at the check-out section.

Offer ends 14th November 2011

Name: ....

Address: ....

....

....

....

Email: ....

DOB: ....

☐ Phase Eight would like to keep you updated from
time to time with new season brochures and details of
promotions by post or email. Please tick this box if you
do not wish this to happen.

☐ Hayhouse, publishers of Many Lives would like to keep
you updated from time to time with news of books and
special offers by post or email. Please tick this box if
you do not wish this to happen.

JOIN THE HAY HOUSE FAMILY

As the leading self-help, mind, body and spirit publisher in the UK, we'd like to welcome you to our family so that you can enjoy all the benefits our website has to offer.

 EXTRACTS from a selection of your favourite author titles

 COMPETITIONS, PRIZES & SPECIAL OFFERS Win extracts, money off, downloads and so much more

 LISTEN to a range of radio interviews and our latest audio publications

 CELEBRATE YOUR BIRTHDAY An inspiring gift will be sent your way

 LATEST NEWS Keep up with the latest news from and about our authors

 ATTEND OUR AUTHOR EVENTS Be the first to hear about our author events

 iPHONE APPS Download your favourite app for your iPhone

 HAY HOUSE INFORMATION Ask us anything, all enquiries answered

join us online at **www.hayhouse.co.uk**

 292B Kensal Road, London W10 5BE
T: 020 8962 1230 E: info@hayhouse.co.uk